MW00368455

Math Logic

By
Q. L. PEARCE

COPYRIGHT © 2007 Mark Twain Media, Inc.

ISBN 978-1-58037-425-5

Printing No. CD-404074

Mark Twain Media, Inc., Publishers
Distributed by Carson-Dellosa Publishing LLC

Visit us at www.carsondellosa.com

226731

Table of Contents

Introduction

Mathematical Thinking

Logic problems are basic to building overall thinking skills, such as problem solving and reasoning. Using clues, students solve real-world problems by comparing facts, making connections, distinguishing necessary information from unnecessary information, drawing logical conclusions, and communicating solutions. The logic problems in this book require students to find patterns and relationships. Learning objectives include development of problem-solving strategies and higher-order thinking skills such as deduction and inference.

These activities have been designed to assist students in meeting the following NCTM standards for problem solving and reasoning:

Problem Solving

* Build new mathematical knowledge through problem solving

* Solve problems that arise in mathematics and in other contexts

* Apply and adapt a variety of appropriate strategies to solve problems

Reasoning and Proof

* Recognize reasoning and proof as fundamental aspects of mathematics

* Select and use various types of reasoning and methods of proof

* Recognize and apply deductive and inductive reasoning

Using This Book

The logic problems are presented in three skill levels from the simplest (one star *) to the most challenging (three stars ***). Instruct students to read the introduction and clues carefully before starting a problem. Let them know that one clue can lead to more than one answer. Suggest that students regularly go back and reread earlier clues, since information in later clues may suggest a connection.

Introduction (cont.)

Strategies for Solving Nonroutine Math Problems

* Look for the use of conditional statements, such as "if this is true, then."

* Organize answers in a list, table, or chart. By keeping track of information, students can compare and contrast facts to determine answers and identify missing data.

* Draw a picture or diagram. For some students, a visual representation can be helpful. Using objects or acting out a problem may also be effective.

* If students need help spatially organizing the clues, there are two different reproducible grids that are provided on page 76 at the back of the book. Students may also draw their own grids.

Use the following warm-up activities to demonstrate problem-solving strategies:

1. Put the following students in order from oldest to youngest.

   Andrew is older than Paul, but younger than Marie. Sue is younger than Andrew, but older than Ann. Ann is older than Paul.

   Answer: Marie, Andrew, Sue, Ann, Paul

2. Determine the order in a race from first to third.

   Sam did not finish first. Angela finished ahead of Bill. Bill did not finish second.

   Answer: Angela, Sam, Bill

3. Match each student to a backpack.

   The backpacks are pink, green, and blue. The girl with the pink backpack sits behind the girl with the blue backpack. Collin sits in the first seat. Beth sits behind Collin and in front of Jill.

   Answer: Collin/green, Beth/blue, Jill/pink

Name: _____ Date: _____

Animal Friends*

Problem: Mrs. Amaya asked her class to write a story about a pet. Use the clues to match each student to his or her pet.

Students: Ryan   Angela   Paul   Anika

Pets: fish   dog   bird   cat

Clues:

1. Anika's pet does not have feathers.

2. Ryan's pet does not swim every day.

3. The dog belongs to a boy.

4. Angela's pet has fur.

5. Ryan's pet does not bark.

Answer: Use the space below to work through the logic problem and write your answers.

_____

_____

_____

_____

_____

_____

_____

_____

_____

Name: _____ Date: _____

Summer Days*

Problem: Six friends are sharing a cabin at summer camp. There are six bunks in each cabin—three upper and three lower. The bunks are numbered 1, 2, and 3 from left to right. Use the clues to learn which boy is in which bunk.

Campers: Ethan   Scott   Fernando   Damon   Mark   Hiroshi

Bunks: upper 1, 2, 3, and lower 1, 2, 3

Clues:

1. The tallest boy has the lower bunk below the shortest boy.

2. Ethan is the youngest boy. He picked a top bunk on the left.

3. Scott has the bunk below Hiroshi.

4. Fernando is the shortest boy.

5. Damon has a bunk below the youngest boy.

6. Scott and Damon are not tall.

7. Hiroshi has a middle bunk to the right of the youngest boy.

Answer: Use the space below to work through the logic problem and write your answers.

_____

_____

_____

_____

_____

_____

_____

_____

_____

Name: _____ Date: _____

And the Winner Is…★

Problem: At the July Fourth Bike Race, there were four entries in the last race. Use the clues to figure out the number for each person and the results of the race.

Entrants: Matthew Vicente Adara Ashley

Numbers: 1 2 3 4

Results: First Second Third Fourth

Clues:
1. Matthew placed lower than Vicente.

2. The person in fourth place wore #2.

3. The racer wearing #3 won.

4. Ashley placed third.

5. Vicente wore #1.

Answer: Use the space below to work through the logic problem and write your answers.

_____

_____

_____

_____

_____

_____

_____

_____

_____

Name: _____ Date: _____

Born in the U.S.A.*

Problem: The Massey family is planning a family reunion. Four of the cousins were born in different states. Follow the clues to find out who comes from which state.

Cousins: Jake   Yanni   Preston   Elise

States: Oklahoma   New York   Florida   California

Clues:

1. Jake was not born in the Midwest.

2. Yanni was born in a coastal city.

3. Preston was born in a state west of where Jake was born.

4. Elise was not born in Florida.

5. Yanni traveled east to attend the reunion in Jake's state.

Answer: Use the space below to work through the logic problem and write your answers.

_____

_____

_____

_____

_____

_____

_____

_____

_____

_____

Name: _____ Date: _____

Zoo Art★

Problem: Mrs. Alonzo's class took a field trip to the zoo. The students were asked to draw a picture of their favorite animal. Use the clues to figure out which animal is in each student's picture.

Students: Amanda   Kayla   David   Adam

Animals: alligator   zebra   giraffe   flamingo

Clues:

1. Adam did not draw a mammal.

2. The animal David drew did not have stripes.

3. Amanda drew an animal that has a long neck, but no feathers.

4. David drew a picture of an animal with many sharp teeth.

Answer: Use the space below to work through the logic problem and write your answers.

_____

_____

_____

_____

_____

_____

_____

_____

_____

_____

Name: _____ Date: _____

At the Movies*

Problem: Five friends wanted to go to a movie on Saturday, but they each had to finish their chores before they could go. Use the clues to determine what time each friend arrived at the theater.

Friends: Amy   Caleb   Jada   Owen   Nick

Arrival Times: 2:00   1:30   1:20   1:50   2:10

Clues:

1. The friends start their chores at noon and the movie starts at 2:00 P.M.

2. Jada had four chores, and each one took twenty minutes. It took ten minutes to get to the theater.

3. Caleb arrived later than Nick.

4. Owen did not arrive first or last.

5. Amy arrived first.

6. Nick was not early or late.

Answer: Use the space below to work through the logic problem and write your answers.

_____

_____

_____

_____

_____

_____

_____

_____

_____

Name: _____ Date: _____

Whirlwind Tour ⋆

Problem: The Marquez Family took a vacation to Europe. They traveled to five countries. Use the clues to determine in which order they visited each nation.

Countries: France   Germany   England   Italy   Sweden

Clues:

1. They did not visit Germany first.

2. They visited Sweden before Italy but after France.

3. They began their trip in a nation that recognizes English as the official language.

4. They took a train from England to France.

5. They visited Germany after Sweden but before Italy.

Answer: Use the space below to work through the logic problem and write your answers.

_____

_____

_____

_____

_____

_____

_____

_____

_____

_____

Name: _____ Date: _____

May I Take Your Coat?*

Problem: When Rachel's mom took her and three friends to a new restaurant, the girls mixed up their coat check numbers. Use the clues to help sort out which number belongs to which girl.

Girls: Rachel   Maria   Karen   Leah

Coat check numbers: 10   21   23   24

Clues:

1. Maria and Leah both had red coats.

2. Karen's number was higher than Rachel's and lower than Maria's.

3. The girl with #23 had a green coat.

4. Rachel had a blue coat.

5. Leah and Maria had even numbers.

Answer: Use the space below to work through the logic problem and write your answers.

_____

_____

_____

_____

_____

_____

_____

_____

_____

_____

Name: _____ Date: _____

Science Skills*

Problem: Mr. Ameche's students are preparing projects for the science fair. Use the clues to match each student with his or her project.

Students: Sofia   Michelle   Devin   Brody   Emilio

Project Topics: volcanoes   plants and light   recycling   magnets   life cycle of a moth

Clues:

1. Brody and the boy with black hair chose projects about living things.

2. The girl who works with magnets is Emilio's sister.

3. Devin and his friend, who is doing the project on recycling, are blondes.

4. Michelle is an only child.

5. Two of Brody's examples escaped from his project.

Answer: Use the space below to work through the logic problem and write your answers.

_____

_____

_____

_____

_____

_____

_____

_____

_____

_____

Name: _____ Date: _____

Fun Fitness*

Problem: Grover School's Field Day included several fitness events. Use the clues to determine who won each event.

Winners: Samantha   Oscar   Saul   Rodrigo   Cher

Activities: push-ups   sit-ups   one-mile run   rope climb   one hundred yard dash

Clues:

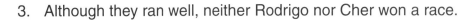

1. Saul came in second in the one-hundred-yard dash and fourth in push-ups.

2. A girl won sit-ups and placed second in push-ups.

3. Although they ran well, neither Rodrigo nor Cher won a race.

4. The winner of the push-ups competition didn't enter any other events.

5. Samantha came in second in sit-ups.

Answer: Use the space below to work through the logic problem and write your answers.

_____

_____

_____

_____

_____

_____

_____

_____

_____

_____

_____

Name: _____ Date: _____

Cake Walk*

Problem: Wilmington School held a bake sale. Use the clues to determine who sold the most goodies and raised the most money.

Volunteers: Alma   Rick   Susan   Pete

Baked Goods: cakes   cookies   cupcakes   pies

Amounts Raised: $50 $100 $80 $55

Clues:

1. Susan did not sell cakes, but she raised more money than the person who did.

2. Alma made twice as much money as the person who sold pies.

3. The person who sold cookies made more than $55.

4. Pete made the least amount of money.

5. Alma's biggest sellers were ginger snaps and chocolate chip.

Answer: Use the space below to work through the logic problem and write your answers.

_____

_____

_____

_____

_____

_____

_____

_____

_____

_____

Name: _____ Date: _____

Dress Up*

Problem: Avon City holds an annual Halloween Costume contest. Use the clues to learn who won and what they wore.

Winners: James   LeVar   Romy   Deanna   Paul

Costumes: mouse   pirate   mummy   rock star   chicken

Clues:

1. LeVar had decided to be a pirate, but changed his mind.

2. Paul wore an animal costume.

3. The girl who wore the rock star costume carried a toy guitar.

4. Deanna and the boy dressed as a pirate are cousins.

5. The person dressed as a chicken and the girl dressed as a mouse applauded when LeVar won his prize.

6. James' sister dressed as a rock star.

Answer: Use the space below to work through the logic problem and write your answers.

_____

_____

_____

_____

_____

_____

_____

_____

_____

Name: _____ Date: _____

Right On Time*

Problem: Tom, the head counselor at Pine Crest Camp, lost his schedule for Saturday. Use the clues to figure out when each activity takes place.

Activities: swimming   hiking   canoeing   crafts   free time

Time: 9:00 A.M.   11:00 A.M.   1:00 P.M.   3:00 P.M.   4:00 P.M.

Clues:

1. The campers have lunch at noon. They do something relaxing after lunch.

2. All lake activities are scheduled for before lunch.

3. Hiking is not the last activity of the day.

4. The first activity of the day is Tom's favorite. His second favorite is canoeing.

5. Tom usually chooses to nap or read a book at 1:00 P.M.

Answer: Use the space below to work through the logic problem and write your answers.

_____

_____

_____

_____

_____

_____

_____

_____

_____

_____

Name: _____ Date: _____

Weather Report*

Problem: Margo keeps a weather journal. She records the temperature and general conditions. Use the clues to figure out what the weather was like from Monday to Friday.

Conditions: sunny   cloudy   drizzle   rain   partly cloudy

Temperatures: 59°   57°   68°   63°   71°

Clues:

1. Wednesday was the coldest, wettest day of the week. It was two degrees colder than Tuesday.

2. It did not rain or drizzle on Monday or Thursday.

3. Thursday was five degrees warmer than Monday.

4. Margo needed her umbrella for two days in a row.

5. The wet weather was clearing on Thursday. Margo needed her sunglasses on Friday.

Answer: Use the space below to work through the logic problem and write your answers.

_____

_____

_____

_____

_____

_____

_____

_____

_____

Name: _____ Date: _____

Pick a Card *

Problem: When Jack got a new bicycle for his birthday, his friends asked for a chance to ride it. To decide the order his friends would ride, Jack asked them each to draw a card. The boy with the highest card went first. Use the clues to determine the order.

Friends: Owen   Antonio   Xavier   Cody   Matt

Cards Drawn: Ace   2   4   7   Queen

Clues:

1. Jack said that an ace would count as one and a picture card as ten.

2. Antonio did not draw a card with a number on it.

3. Owen did not win. His card was higher than Matt's and lower than Cody's.

4. Xavier rode before Antonio but after Cody.

5. Owen rode third.

Answer: Use the space below to work through the logic problem and write your answers.

_____

_____

_____

_____

_____

_____

_____

_____

_____

_____

Name: _____ Date: _____

Class Favorites*

Problem: Joshua and his friends each have a favorite subject in school. Use the clues to match each student with his or her favorite subject.

Students: Joshua   Grace   Kyle   Maria   Tammy

Subjects: math   science   reading   art   social studies

Clues:

1. Maria's best friend loves art.

2. Tammy's brother likes reading.

3. Kyle does not enjoy social studies, and he does not have a sister.

4. Maria likes math and social studies, but they are not her favorites.

5. Tammy's best friend is Maria.

Answer: Use the space below to work through the logic problem and write your answers.

Name: _____ Date: _____

Tournament Time*

Problem: When the city soccer tournament was over, Wesley helped his dad add up the scores and make a list of the final standings. Use the clues to determine what the standings were.

Teams: Razors   Hot Shots   Tigers   Gold Rush
Dragons   Storm   Gators

Clues:

1. The Gold Rush finished behind the Hot Shots and ahead of the Tigers and the Storm.

2. The Razors and the Storm were not in last place.

3. The Tigers finished fifth ahead of the Razors.

4. The Dragons finished higher than the Razors and the Storm, but were not second or fourth.

Answer: Use the space below to work through the logic problem and write your answers.

_____

_____

_____

_____

_____

_____

_____

_____

_____

_____

_____

Name: _____ Date: _____

Farm Fresh★

Problem: On Wednesday, there were four deliveries at the Farmer's Market. Use the clues to figure out what each person delivered in what order.

Names: Jim   Angelo   Tom   Warren

Deliveries: tomatoes   lettuce   onions   strawberries

Order: first   second   third   fourth

Clues:

1. Jim arrived at the market second, after the man who delivers strawberries. He did not deliver tomatoes.

2. The man who delivers onions drives a black pickup truck. He arrived last.

3. Warren, who drives a white van, used to deliver strawberries but he changed jobs.

4. Tom drives a blue van. He did not arrive third.

Answer: Use the space below to work through the logic problem and write your answers.

_____

_____

_____

_____

_____

_____

_____

_____

_____

Name: _____ Date: _____

 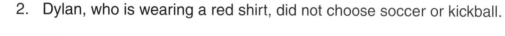

A Friendly Game*

Problem: Dylan and a few other students wanted to start a game at recess. They couldn't agree on what to play. Use the clues to determine who wanted to play what.

Students: Dylan   Zeke   Rose   Zoe   Sonny

Games: kickball   tetherball   handball   soccer   dodgeball

Clues:

1. Zeke is older than Sonny and Rose, who is not the youngest.

2. Dylan, who is wearing a red shirt, did not choose soccer or kickball.

3. The oldest student, a boy who is wearing a blue shirt, chose dodgeball.

4. The youngest girl chose tetherball.

5. A girl chose soccer.

Answer: Use the space below to work through the logic problem and write your answers.

_____

_____

_____

_____

_____

_____

_____

_____

_____

_____

Name: _____ Date: _____

Who's Next?*

Problem: Five children each have dentist appointments. Use the clues to learn the order of the appointments.

Children: Benjamin   Robert   Chelsea   Amy   Brook

Appointments: 10:00 A.M.   11:00 A.M.   1:00 P.M.   2:00 P.M.   3:00 P.M.

Clues:

1. Chelsea's appointment is before Brook's and after 11:00 A.M.

2. A girl has the first appointment.

3. Benjamin has an afternoon appointment.

4. Brook does not have the last appointment.

Answer: Use the space below to work through the logic problem and write your answers.

_____

_____

_____

_____

_____

_____

_____

_____

_____

_____

Name: _____ Date: _____

Beach Day★

Problem: It's Beach Day for Carla's youth group. How many students are in Carla's group and how many supplies did the group bring?

Supplies: sandwiches   drinks   cookies   beach balls   beach blankets

Clues:

1. They brought two sandwiches per person.

2. They brought half as many drinks as cookies.

3. They brought one beach ball for every five children.

4. They brought one beach blanket for every three children.

5. Each child had two drinks.

6. They brought 30 chocolate chip and 30 oatmeal cookies.

Answer: Use the space below to work through the logic problem and write your answers.

_____

_____

_____

_____

_____

_____

_____

_____

_____

_____

Name: _____ Date: _____

Summer Party★

Problem: Alejandro planned a summer party for his friends. Use the clues to determine how many friends he invited and the cost per guest.

Expenses: refreshments   decorations   party favors

Clues:

1. Alejandro invited 25 percent of his class.

2. There were fewer than 30 students in Alejandro's class.

3. The refreshments were half the cost of the party.

4. The decorations cost 21 dollars.

5. Each guest received a party favor that cost two dollars.

6. The number of students in the class can be evenly divided by seven and 14.

Answer: Use the space below to work through the logic problem and write your answers.

_____

_____

_____

_____

_____

_____

_____

_____

_____

_____

Name: _____ Date: _____

Game Time*

Problem: During recess, Austin and his friends played basketball. Use the clues to determine how many points each student scored.

Players: Austin   Sawyer   Jacob   David

Points Scored: 20   12   6   10

Clues: 1. The players earned two points for each basket.

2. David made more than three baskets.

3. Austin scored more points than Sawyer.

4. Sawyer scored half as many points as Jacob.

5. David scored twice as many points as Austin.

Answer: Use the space below to work through the logic problem and write your answers.

_____

_____

_____

_____

_____

_____

_____

_____

_____

Name: _____ Date: _____

A Field Trip*

Problem: The fifth-grade classes at Whittington Elementary took a trip to the museum. Use the clues to determine how many buses they needed, how many miles they drove for the round trip to and from the museum, and at what time they arrived back at school.

Classes: Mr. Domenoske (23 students)
Mrs. Corwin (31 students)
Mrs. May (27 students)

Clues:

1. The corner of Elm Avenue and Main Street is 11 miles from the museum.

2. Mrs. May's entire class rode on one bus.

3. The class was at the museum for three hours.

4. The bus started on Grover Street, drove eight miles, and then went six miles on Main Street to Elm Avenue.

5. The bus drove an average of 30 miles per hour.

6. Four of Mrs. Corwin's students rode on the bus with Mr. Domenoske's class.

7. The class left for the museum at 8:30 A.M.

Answer: Use the space below to work through the logic problem and write your answers.

_____

_____

_____

_____

_____

_____

_____

_____

Name: _____ Date: _____

Gifts Galore★★

Problem: Jenna is having a birthday party. Use the clues to match each guest to the gift he or she brought.

Guests: Patrick   Ruby   Amanda   Nicole   Keenan

Gifts: CD   book   puzzle   candy   gift certificate

Clues:

1. Ruby and the girl who brought the puzzle arrived early.

2. The boy in the blue shirt brought candy.

3. The girl who brought the CD had two pieces of cake.

4. Amanda arrived with the girl who brought the gift certificate.

5. Keenan is wearing a red shirt.

6. Amanda and Ruby did not eat cake.

7. Keenan arrived with Nicole.

Answer: Use the space below to work through the logic problem and write your answers.

_____

_____

_____

_____

_____

_____

_____

_____

_____

Name: _____ Date: _____

*Weekend Work***

Problem: Robin started his own business doing odd jobs for neighbors. Use the clues to find out which side of the street and in what order the neighborhood's houses are, what Robin's last name is, and what jobs he does for each neighbor.

Neighbors: Schumans   Carters   Shaws   Feltons   Trujillos   Mercados

Jobs: mow lawn   walk dog   feed fish   water plants   babysit

Location: north side of the street   south side of the street

Clues:
1. The Mercados live at the northwest end of the street.

2. Robin walks the dog for the people who live directly south of the Carters.

3. Robin feeds the fish for the family living west of the Shaws.

4. The Trujillos do not have a dog.

5. Robin's family lives between the Mercados and the people who ask him to babysit.

6. Robin mows the lawn for the family south of the Shaws.

7. The Schumans live west of the Trujillos and south of the Mercados.

Answer: Use the space below to work through the logic problem and write your answers.

_____

_____

_____

_____

_____

_____

_____

_____

Name: _____ Date: _____

At the Fair★★

Problem: Four students have volunteered to help out at the school fair. They each work in a different place, and they each wear a shirt of a different color. Use the clues to determine where each student works and the color of his or her shirt.

Students: Aaron   Ann   Chloe   Randy

Jobs: games   rides   petting zoo   food service

Colors: red   yellow   green   blue

Clues:

1. A girl is helping with rides.
2. Randy is wearing a blue shirt.
3. Aaron is not helping with games.
4. Chloe does not have a yellow shirt.
5. Ann is wearing a red shirt.
6. The girl helping with the petting zoo is not wearing red.
7. The boy wearing yellow is helping with food.

Answer: Use the space below to work through the logic problem and write your answers.

_____

_____

_____

_____

_____

_____

_____

_____

_____

Name: _____ Date: _____

Family Matters★★

Problem: Grady and his three friends have a lot in common. They each have one brother and one sister. Use the clues to determine who belongs to which family.

Friends: Grady   Daniel   Anthony   Tyler

Brothers: Brandon   Austin   Nathan   Carlos

Sisters: Kelsey   Ana   Haley   Marissa

Clues:

1. Tyler's sister and Kelsey are in the same class. They are best friends.

2. Haley's brother is three years older than she is. He is a goalie on the eighth-grade soccer team.

3. Grady's brother, Austin, is in high school. He is in the same grade as Daniel's brother.

4. Brandon is in the eighth grade.

5. Carlos is a forward on the same soccer team as Haley's brother. His sister is sixteen.

6. Haley often goes to the movies with her best friend, Kelsey.

7. Ana is three years old.

8. Nathan is in high school.

9. Sometimes Kelsey babysits for Daniel's little sister.

Answer: Use the space below to work through the logic problem and write your answers.

_____

_____

_____

_____

_____

_____

_____

     28

Name: _____   Date: _____

The Play Is the Thing **

Problem: Mr. Jagellio's class is performing a play. Use the clues to figure out which part each student has.

Students: Christopher   William   Alexander   Emma   Mary

Parts: toymaker   mayor   toy soldier   cook   musician

Clues:
1. Mr. Jagellio chose the shortest student to play the mayor.
2. Neither Mary nor Emma can play an instrument.
3. The students who play the toymaker and the cook are brother and sister.
4. Mary does not play the mayor.
5. William does not have a sister.
6. A blonde girl has the part of the toy soldier.
7. Christopher and William are both tall.
8. The student who plays the toymaker plays piano.
9. Alexander is an only child.
10. Mary has brown hair.

Answer: Use the space below to work through the logic problem and write your answers.

_____

_____

_____

_____

_____

_____

_____

_____

_____

_____

29

Name: _____ Date: _____

On the Field ★★

Problem: The name of Lucas' soccer team is the Stars. Four of his team members live in the same apartment building as Lucas. Use the clues to figure out which positions Lucas and his neighbors play.

Boys: Lucas   Sean   Joe   Ian   Mark

Positions: forward   goalie   fullback   sweeper   left wing

Clues:

1. Sean is not a forward. His best friend is the left wing.

2. The youngest boy lives on the third floor, two floors above Lucas.

3. The sweeper's best friend is Joe.

4. The goalie and Mark are best friends.

5. The forward lives on the third floor.

6. The boy who lives on the first floor is the goalie.

7. Ian is the youngest. His best friend does not play soccer.

Answer: Use the space below to work through the logic problem and write your answers.

_____

_____

_____

_____

_____

_____

_____

_____

_____

Name: _____ Date: _____

Practice Makes Perfect ★★

Problem: Priscilla and her older sister are training for a bike race. On Saturday they go for a practice ride. Use the clues to figure out what streets they take, how far they ride on each street, and the order of the streets.

Streets: Atlanta   Willow   Regent   Pine   Brookside

Distances: 1.5 miles   2 miles   3 miles   3.5 miles   4 miles

Clues:

1. They rode further on Brookside than on Pine.

2. They rode further on Atlanta than Regent.

3. Priscilla chose to do the shortest stretch first, then turn onto Brookside.

4. They rode the 4-mile stretch before the 3.5-mile stretch.

5. They rode the last 2 miles on Pine.

6. They rode further on Regent than on Brookside.

Answer: Use the space below to work through the logic problem and write your answers.

_____

_____

_____

_____

_____

_____

_____

_____

_____

_____

Name: _____ Date: _____

Summer Reading★★

Problem: Last summer, José and Meena spent a week with their grandparents. During the week they each read four books. Use the clues to discover who read which books and in what order.

Readers: José   Meena

Books:
Stormy (mystery)   *The Funny Guy* (humor)   *Later That Day* (horror)
Spring (fantasy)   *Hill Street* (action)   *The First Robin* (nonfiction)
The Mystery of King Lake (mystery)   *The Fear Speaker* (sci-fi)

Clues:

1. Meena likes mysteries.
2. The title of the fourth book he read reminded José of his school.
3. Meena enjoys humor, but she didn't read a humorous book.
4. José did not read a book with a one-word title.
5. Meena saved her nonfiction book for last.
6. José and Meena attend the Hill Street School.
7. Meena read the fantasy before she read *The Mystery of King Lake*.
8. José did not start with a scary book. He read *The Fear Speaker* after the scary book.
9. Meena read *Stormy* third.

Answer: Use the space below to work through the logic problem and write your answers.

_____

_____

_____

_____

_____

_____

_____

_____

Name: _____ Date: _____

Spooky Tales★★

Problem: Telling scary stories is a favorite pastime for Nina and her friends. Use the clues to figure out each storyteller's setting and scary main character.

Story Teller: Nina   Andrew   Noah   Emily   Nicolas

Character: ghost   mummy   werewolf   zombie   vampire

Setting: old house   swamp   empty school   cemetery   shopping mall

Clues:

1. Noah pictured his character in a darkened classroom
2. The ghost story is not set in an old building or a cemetery.
3. Nicolas wanted to do a vampire story, but he changed his mind.
4. Nina's character does not drink blood, but it does have sharp teeth and fur.
5. Emily set her story in an outdoor place, but not a swamp.
6. Andrew did not tell about a zombie or a mummy.
7. A girl told the mummy story.
8. Nina and Andrew did not use an outdoor setting.
9. The werewolf story was not set in an old house.

Answer: Use the space below to work through the logic problem and write your answers.

_____

_____

_____

_____

_____

_____

_____

_____

Name: _____ Date: _____

*Perfect Pizza***

Problem: Marcus and his friends got together to work on a school project. When they ordered pizza, everyone wanted different toppings. They decided to share three large pizzas with two toppings on each. Use the clues to determine the three different topping combinations and who shared which pizza.

Friends: Marcus Dimitri Tai Harry Melanie Holly

Toppings: mushrooms onions sausage pepperoni peppers double cheese

Clues:
1. Tai does not eat meat.
2. Holly will not eat peppers.
3. Pizza #1 combines double cheese and pepperoni.
4. Dimitri loves mushrooms. He doesn't mind peppers, but he would prefer not to have onions.
5. Two people like sausage. One of them shared a pizza with Marcus.
6. Melanie likes sausage and pepperoni.
7. Pizza #2 combines mushrooms and peppers.
8. Melanie does not like onions or mushrooms. Marcus likes onions a lot and Harry doesn't mind them.

Answer: Use the space below to work through the logic problem and write your answers.

_____

_____

_____

_____

_____

_____

_____

_____

_____

_____

Name: _____ Date: _____

New Friends★★

Problem: The local pet supply store held an Adopt-a-Pet Day. There were three dogs and three cats at the store and they all found new homes. Use the clues to discover which family adopted which pet and whether the pet is a dog or cat.

Pet Names: Max   Blue   Woodrow   Angel   Tucker   Mischief

Family Names: Rogers   Shindri   Coffman   Stein   Rodriguez   Wolf

Clues:
1. Angel is the only female cat.
2. The Wolf family adopted a dog, but not Blue, the male Chihuahua.
3. The Rogers family already has a dog but no cat. They adopted a male cat.
4. Tucker is young black labrador.
5. A family with two cats adopted Woodrow.
6. Mischief is an older coonhound.
5. The Coffmans adopted a small male dog.
7. The Shindri family did not have any pets.
8. The Rogers family did not adopt a dog, but the Rodriguez family did.
9. The Wolf family adopted an older pet.

Answer: Use the space below to work through the logic problem and write your answers.

_____

_____

_____

_____

_____

_____

_____

_____

_____

_____

Name: _____ Date: _____

Gift Exchange★★

Problem: For a holiday, the girls in Nancy's dance class decided to draw names for a gift exchange. Use the clues to determine to whom each girl gave each gift.

Girls: Nancy   Reba   Lonnie   Isabel   Venisha

Gifts: book   hair clips   lip gloss   bubble bath   chocolates

Clues:

1. Lonnie drew the name of the youngest girl.
2. Venisha did not receive an edible gift.
3. Isabel is younger than Nancy and older than Reba.
4. Nancy did not draw Venisha's name.
5. Isabel gave lip gloss to the oldest girl.
6. Lonnie received a book from the girl to whom she gave a gift.
7. Venisha, who is older than Lonnie, gave bubble bath.
8. Lonnie gave an edible gift.
9. Nancy is not the oldest girl.

Answer: Use the space below to work through the logic problem and write your answers.

_____

_____

_____

_____

_____

_____

_____

_____

_____

Name: _____ Date: _____

Good Morning ★★

Problem: Michael and his family went to a restaurant for Sunday breakfast, and everyone had something different to eat and drink. Use the clues to discover what each person had.

Family: Michael   Taryn   Lizbeth   Mom   Dad

Meals: eggs and toast   cereal   omelet   waffles with strawberry syrup   pancakes with maple syrup

Drinks: orange juice   tea   coffee   milk   tomato juice

Clues:
1. Dad had an egg dish, but Michael did not.
2. Mom did not have syrup.
3. Michael did not drink juice or coffee.
4. The person who had the omelet drank tomato juice.
5. Mom did not have a hot breakfast, but she did have a hot drink.
6. Lizbeth does not like maple syrup.
7. The person who had eggs and toast drank tea.
8. Dad had juice.
9. Lizbeth did not have milk or tea.

Answer: Use the space below to work through the logic problem and write your answers.

_____

_____

_____

_____

_____

_____

_____

_____

_____

Name: _____ Date: _____

Pick a Number★★

Problem: Five students in Mrs. Arnold's class wanted to take care of the class hamster over the weekend. Mrs. Arnold wrote a number on a piece of paper. She asked each student to think of a number between one and 50, and the one who came closest to hers would take the hamster home. Use the clues to figure out which numbers the students and Mrs. Arnold picked. Who took the hamster home?

People: Luke   Riley   Adam   Cameron   Lucia   Mrs. Arnold

Numbers: 33   12   45   30   22   17

Clues:

1. Luke's number could not be divided by ten or 11.
2. Mrs. Arnold picked an even number.
3. Adam's number could be divided by five.
4. Luke's number was lower than Adam's.
5. Riley's number was higher than Mrs. Arnold's number.
6. Lucia and Adam picked odd numbers.
7. Cameron has a lower number than Mrs. Arnold.
8. Riley's number could be divided by three but not ten.

Answer: Use the space below to work through the logic problem and write your answers.

_____

_____

_____

_____

_____

_____

_____

_____

_____

Name: _____ Date: _____

On Stage★★

Problem: The drama club sold tickets to the Saturday performances of the school play. Use the clues to figure out how many tickets were sold on each day and for which performance.

Performances: afternoon   evening

Sales Days: Monday   Tuesday   Wednesday   Thursday

Tickets Sold: 35   30   45   20   100   55   75   40

Clues:

1. Wednesday was the only day when students sold more afternoon than evening tickets.
2. The highest number of afternoon tickets were sold on Tuesday.
3. Fewer evening tickets were sold on Wednesday than Thursday.
4. On Thursday, sales for afternoon tickets were half those of evening tickets.
5. The highest ticket sales for any performance were on Tuesday.
6. Ten more tickets were sold for the afternoon performance on Wednesday than on Monday.
7. The second highest ticket sales for any performance were sold on Monday.
8. Students sold 35 afternoon tickets on Monday.

Answer: Use the space below to work through the logic problem and write your answers.

_____

_____

_____

_____

_____

_____

_____

_____

Name: _____ Date: _____

In the Bank**

Problem: Anisa has four animal-shaped banks, each of a different color. She is saving up for four different things. Use the clues to determine what animal is which color bank, how much change is in each bank, and for what Anisa is saving.

Colors: pink   blue   yellow   green

Animals: pig   kitten   bunny   puppy

Amounts: $5.74 $10.03 $3.17 $14.22

Purpose: candy   a pet rat   a rainy day   a gift for her mom

Clues:
1. There is more in the blue bank than the yellow bank and less in the blue bank than the green bank.
2. Anisa saved more money for a rainy day than for candy.
3. The money for her pet rat is in the kitten bank.
4. There is $10.03 in the green puppy bank.
5. She keeps her candy money in her pig bank.
6. The bunny bank holds the most money.
7. Her kitten bank is blue.
8. The money for her mom's gift is not in the green bank.
9. The pig bank is not pink.

Answer: Use the space below to work through the logic problem and write your answers.

_____

_____

_____

_____

_____

_____

_____

_____

_____

Name: _____ Date: _____

The Winning Ticket★★

Problem: At the school fair, Wendy sold raffle tickets to five of her neighbors. Each neighbor won something. Use the clues to figure out how many tickets each neighbor bought and what he or she won.

Neighbors: Mr. Bates   Ms. Amos   Mr. Hunter   Mr. Perch   Mrs. Heinz

Prizes: movie tickets   blender   plant   stuffed bear   roller blades

Number of tickets: 1   3   5   6   10

Clues:
1. The person who bought 10 tickets won roller blades.
2. Mr. Hunter bought more tickets than Ms. Amos.
3. Mr. Bates did not win movie tickets.
4. The person who won the blender bought more tickets than Mr. Bates.
5. Mrs. Heinz bought fewer tickets than the woman who won the bear, but more than Mr. Bates.
6. Mr. Bates did not buy 10 tickets.
7. Mr. Perch could not put his prize in his pocket.
8. The man who won the blender gave it to his mother.
9. Mr. Hunter did not buy the most or the least tickets.

Answer: Use the space below to work through the logic problem and write your answers.

_____

_____

_____

_____

_____

_____

_____

_____

_____

_____

Name: _____ Date: _____

Spelling Bee★★

Problem: Mr. Annan's class had a spelling bee. Use the clues to determine in what order the students competed, which student misspelled which word, and which student won.

Students: Collin   Alisha   Tom   Arthur   Briana

Words: psychology   asteroid   barnacle   gadget   correspond

Order: 1st   2nd   3rd   4th   5th

Clues:

1. Alisha, who was first in line, misspelled an eight-letter word.
2. The girl who was third in line misspelled *gadget.*
3. Tom did not spell his word correctly.
4. Collin was not second in line.
5. The fourth student in line was the winner.
6. Arthur misspelled a ten-letter word.
7. The boy who was fifth in line misspelled the word *barnacle.*
8. Collin's word was not last alphabetically.

Answer: Use the space below to work through the logic problem and write your answers.

_____

_____

_____

_____

_____

_____

_____

_____

_____

Name: _____ Date: _____

Snack Attack★★

Problem: Zoey, Rose, and Haley went to a movie on Saturday. Read the clues to find out what drinks and snacks each girl had and how much they each spent for their tickets, drinks, and snacks.

Girls: Zoey   Rose   Haley

Snacks: popcorn   candy   nachos

Drinks: soda   juice   water

Clues:

1. Zoey spent the most money.

2. Rose had a two-dollar discount coupon for her ticket.

3. The candy cost two-thirds as much as nachos and twice as much as popcorn.

4. The girl who had water did not spend the least.

5. The final total for the tickets was thirteen dollars.

6. The girl who bought nachos also bought juice.

7. Soda and juice cost the same as candy and twice as much as water.

8. The least expensive snack cost one dollar.

9. Rose's snack cost half as much as her drink.

Answer: Use the space below to work through the logic problem and write your answers.

_____

_____

_____

_____

_____

_____

_____

_____

Name: _____ Date: _____

Teaming Up★★

Problem: Mrs. Talerant divided her class into three teams for a math decathlon. The captains are Ruth, Nelson, and José. Use the clues to figure out how many students are in Mrs. Talerant's class and how many boys and girls are on each team.

Captains: Ruth   Nelson   José

Clues:

1. There are fewer than 40 students in the class.

2. Half the class, less one, are girls.

3. One-quarter of the boys are on Ruth's team.

4. There are an equal number of students on each team.

5. There are an odd number of girls on Nelson and José's teams.

6. The total number of students can be divided by two, three, five, ten, and 15.

7. There are four fewer girls than boys on José's team.

8. The number of boys and girls on Nelson's team is equal.

Answer: Use the space below to work through the logic problem and write your answers.

_____

_____

_____

_____

_____

_____

_____

_____

_____

_____

Name: _____ Date: _____

Shopping Spree★★

Problem: Emma and her friends are shopping at the mall. Use the clues to determine how much money each girl gets as an allowance, the amount each girl started with, and the balance they each have left after shopping.

Girls: Emma   Megan   Latoya

Allowance: $10 per week $10.50 per week $12 per week

Clues:

1. Emma had saved two weeks' allowance for the shopping trip.

2. Megan only bought a sweater that was 50% off the original price of $30.

3. Latoya receives a greater allowance than Emma.

4. Megan saved half of her allowance for six weeks for the shopping trip.

5. Emma spent $12.00 on a gift for her mother. She bought a hair band for $3.00 and a belt for $5.00.

6. Latoya spent one-fourth of her money on a wallet. Then she spent half of what she had left on a pair of shoes.

7. Emma had a balance of $1.00.

8. Latoya had $3.00 more than Megan when they left the mall.

Answer: Use the space below to work through the logic problem and write your answers.

_____

_____

_____

_____

_____

_____

_____

_____

_____

Name: _____ Date: _____

A Pack of Puppies★★

Problem: Sean's dog had five puppies. He found homes for all of them. Use the clues to figure out which puppy went to which family and how much each puppy weighed.

Puppies : Shiloh   Chelsea   Tramp   Stitch   Chatelet

Weights: 5 pounds $5\frac{1}{2}$ pounds   6 pounds $7\frac{1}{2}$ pounds   8 pounds

Families: Cooper   Capaldi   Sullivan   Guerrero

Clues:

1. There are three female and two male puppies.
2. The Coopers adopted two female puppies.
3. Shiloh is the smallest puppy.
4. Stitch and Tramp are both males.
5. The Guerreros adopted Chelsea.
6. The Capaldis adopted the largest puppy.
7. Chatelet weighs two pounds less than Stitch.
8. The Sullivans' puppy weighs $1\frac{1}{2}$ pounds more than Chelsea.

Answer: Use the space below to work through the logic problem and write your answers.

_____

_____

_____

_____

_____

_____

_____

_____

_____

Name: _____ Date: _____

Travis' Bookcase★★★

Problem: Travis loves to read. His favorite kinds of books are mysteries, biographies, adventure, and nonfiction. His bookcase has five shelves. What type of books and how many are on each shelf?

Clues:

1. One-third of the books are mysteries.

2. There are twice as many books on the second from the top shelf as on the third shelf.

3. The adventure books are on a shelf above the biographies.

4. The mysteries are on two shelves, one directly above the other.

5. There are the same number of books on the top and third shelves.

6. There are a total of 42 books.

7. There are no books above nonfiction.

8. There are six books on the third shelf.

9. The biographies are on a shelf below the mysteries.

Answer: Use the space below to work through the logic problem and write your answers.

_____

_____

_____

_____

_____

_____

_____

_____

Name: _____ Date: _____

Running for Office★★★

Problem: In the school elections, four students were voted into office. Use the clues to learn the last name of each winner and the office he or she will fill.

First Names: Tanya   Alexis   Bud   Craig

Last Names: Thomas   Baggins   Wilson   Harlow

Office: President   Vice President   Treasurer   Secretary

Clues:

1. The only student elected who plays soccer is the secretary.
2. The president's last name is Harlow.
3. The vice president is a girl.
4. Tanya's last name is Baggins.
5. The student whose favorite hobby is robotics does not live next door to another student.
6. Craig is not on a sports team.
7. The person with the last name of Thomas lives next door to the treasurer.
8. Alexis Wilson's favorite hobby is photography.
9. Craig does not live next door to another student.
10. Craig's favorite hobby is rock collecting.

Answer: Use the space below to work through the logic problem and write your answers.

_____

_____

_____

_____

_____

_____

_____

_____

_____

Name: _____ Date: _____

Author, Author★★★

Problem: The local bookstore held a contest for young writers. Use the clues to determine the name, age, story, and place for each winner.

Writers: Bethany   Ahmed   Joshua   Gina

Age: 10   11   12   14

Story: "Pig Sty"   "Gone"   "Smooth Hands"   "The Top of the World"

Place: First   Second   Third   Fourth

Clues:
1. Joshua is two years older than the person who came in second.
2. Bethany is two years older than the person who placed fourth.
3. "Gone" didn't win first or second place.
4. Ahmed was neither the youngest nor the oldest writer.
5. "The Top of the World," by the youngest writer, was the only nonfiction entry.
6. The person who came first was not Gina.
7. "Pig Sty" was higher than "The Top of the World" but lower than "Smooth Hands."
8. Ahmed placed higher than Bethany.
9. Joshua placed higher than the youngest writer, but lower than the 11-year-old.
10. The story "Smooth Hands" placed higher than "Gone" and "The Top of the World."

Answer: Use the space below to work through the logic problem and write your answers.

_____

_____

_____

_____

_____

_____

_____

Name: _____ Date: _____

Picture Perfect★★★

Problem: Jenna loves to paint. Her parents have hung four of her best paintings in different rooms of the house. Use the clues to discover which painting is in which room, what medium was used, and in what color frame it is placed.

Paintings: farm scene   bowl of apples   lake scene   self-portrait

Rooms: living room   kitchen   dining room   den

Frame colors: blue   red   green   brown

Mediums: watercolor   oils

Clues:
1. Two of the paintings were done with watercolor.
2. The watercolor painting in the den has a green frame.
3. The painting with the brown frame is in the dining room.
4. The painting in the dining room was not done in watercolor.
5. Jenna's favorite painting is in a red frame.
6. Jenna painted the self-portrait in oils.
7. The bowl of apples is Jenna's favorite painting.
8. The painting in the blue frame is a watercolor.
9. There is an oil painting in the kitchen.
10. The lake painting is in the living room.

Answer: Use the space below to work through the logic problem and write your answers.

_____

_____

_____

_____

_____

_____

_____

_____

Name: _____ Date: _____

Makeover ★★★

Problem: Niecy and her friends each decided to redecorate their rooms. Use the clues to figure out the color and theme of each girl's room.

Girls: Niecy   Hannah   Samantha   Kenshi

Colors: blue   green   pink   yellow

Theme: sports   drama   dance   music

Clues:

1. Samantha and Kenshi do not like pink.
2. The girl with the yellow room is into sports.
3. Niecy did not paint her room yellow.
4. The girl with the music theme sings and plays piano.
5. Kenshi thinks the girl with the drama theme picked a pretty color.
6. Hannah and the girl with the green room have dogs but no cats.
7. Niecy's brother and the girl who likes dance helped Niecy paint her room.
8. The girl with the blue room likes to sing but cannot play an instrument.
9. The girl who picked the drama theme has a cat.
10. The girl with the music theme and the girl with the pink room have sisters but no brothers.
11. Samantha's room is not yellow.
12. The girl with the dance theme tried blue paint, but changed her mind.

Answer: Use the space below to work through the logic problem and write your answers.

_____

_____

_____

_____

_____

_____

_____

_____

_____

_____

Name: _____ Date: _____

Victory Lunch ***

Problem: The swim team celebrated a successful swim meet with lunch at a family restaurant. Use the clues to determine where each team member sat and what he or she had to eat.

Swim Team: James   Dylan   Ben   Justin   Bella   Alyssa   Lauren   Mai

Seats: Table One: A, B, C, D   Table Two: A, B, C, D

Meals: hamburger   salad   chili   fish sticks   veggie burger   chicken strips

Clues:

1. There were two boys and two girls at each table.
2. Both vegetarians were at the same table.
3. Two people ordered hamburgers and two people ordered salads, but only one hamburger and one salad were served at each table.
4. James and Dylan are twins, but Dylan is a vegetarian. James is not.
5. The person in seat A at Table One had fish sticks.
6. The boy in seat A at Table Two had chicken strips. He did not win a race.
7. The girl at Table One had the fastest time in freestyle. She had a hamburger.
8. Alyssa sat in seat B at Table Two. She did not have a salad.
9. The boy with the fastest time in backstroke had chili.
10. James and Dylan sat at different tables.
11. At each table there was a girl who was eating a salad.
12. Unlike Table One, the girls at Table Two sat across from each other.
13. Ben sat in Seat B across from a girl.
14. The boy who had the fastest time in breaststroke had a veggie burger.
15. James did not have the winning time in any event.
16. Lauren is the only girl to win a race. Her best friend, Bella, sat in Seat C.

Answer: Use the space below to work through the logic problem and write your answers.

_____

_____

_____

_____

_____

_____

_____

Name: _____ Date: _____

Saturday Sundae★★★

Problem: Micah and his family went out for ice cream. Use the clues to discover which flavors and toppings each person chose.

Family: Micah   Taylor   P.J.   Mom   Dad

Flavors: vanilla   chocolate   strawberry

Toppings: hot fudge   caramel   rainbow   strawberry   whipped
                                     sprinkles   syrup   cream

Clues:
1. Three people had sprinkles.
2. Two people had chocolate ice cream and two had vanilla ice cream.
3. Taylor and Mom were the only ones who did not have whipped cream.
4. Micah was the only person who had three toppings. He did not have strawberry ice cream.
5. Mom and Taylor had one topping each. Mom was the only person who had strawberry syrup.
6. The person who had strawberry ice cream did not have any syrup.
7. The people who had chocolate ice cream had two toppings each. One had it with caramel.
8. Taylor had sprinkles only.
9. Dad was not the person who had hot fudge.
10. P.J. had sprinkles.

Answer: Use the space below to work through the logic problem and write your answers.

_____

_____

_____

_____

_____

_____

_____

_____

Cool Cash★★★

Problem: To earn extra money, Adrian and his friends are doing yard work on Saturdays. Use the clues to figure out the total they earned, what fraction of the total work hours each boy worked, and how much each boy earned by the end of the summer.

Boys: Adrian   Kevin   Jason   Brandon

Customers: the Clarks   the Onnessis   the Goldbergs

Clues: 1. Adrian and Kevin each worked eight Saturdays.

2. The boys spent one hour every week at the Clarks for eight weeks.

3. The customers paid 12 dollars per hour for the yard work.

4. Jason only worked the four Saturdays that the Goldbergs were scheduled.

5. The boys spent two hours every week at the Onnessis for eight weeks.

6. They spent two hours at the Goldbergs every other week.

7. Brandon only worked four Saturdays. He did not work at the Goldbergs.

Answer: Use the space below to work through the logic problem and write your answers.

_____

_____

_____

_____

_____

_____

_____

_____

_____

_____

Name: _____ Date: _____

My Space***

Problem: Kathleen, Eva, Leah, and Abby decided to figure out who had the largest bedroom. They each measured the length and width of their own room. Use the clues to match each girl to the correct measurements and determine who has the largest room in square feet, and the perimeter and area of each room.

Girls: Kathleen   Eva   Leah   Abby

Length: 14 feet   14 feet   16 feet   18 feet

Width: 10 feet   12 feet   12 feet   14 feet

Clues:
1. Eva's room is two feet longer than it is wide.

2. The perimeter of Leah's room is four feet longer than the perimeter of Kathleen's room.

3. The second largest room is square.

4. The square footage of Abby's room is 160 square feet.

5. Leah's room is 12 feet wide.

Answer: Use the space below to work through the logic problem and write your answers.

_____

_____

_____

_____

_____

_____

_____

_____

_____

_____

Name: _____ Date: _____

In the Garden***

Problem: Ms. Kelly's fifth-grade class planted a vegetable garden at school. The garden has eight rows, each 20 feet long. Use the clues to figure out which vegetables are in which rows and how many plants are in each row.

Vegetables: tomatoes   green peppers   carrots   corn   cucumbers   lettuce

Clues:
1. The corn will grow the tallest.
2. The lettuce plants are 15 inches apart.
3. There are two rows of tomatoes.
4. The carrots are in the second row.
5. Cucumbers are planted one foot apart.
6. Rows seven and eight are for the tallest plants.
7. The plants in rows five and six are the same and about three feet apart.
8. Cucumbers and corn are planted the same distance apart.
9. The plants in the third row are 18 inches apart.
10. Carrots are planted four inches apart between the lettuce and the green peppers.
11. There are 13 plants in the third row.

Answer: Use the space below to work through the logic problem and write your answers.

_____

_____

_____

_____

_____

_____

_____

_____

_____

Name: _____ Date: _____

Earth Friendly ★★★

Problem: On Earth Day, Charlie and his friends each led a team to help clear litter from several large vacant lots. Use the clues to determine how many people were on each team, how many pounds of trash each team collected, and what percentage of their trash was made up of cans, glass, plastic, and paper.

Team Leaders: Charlie   Neville   Yolanda   Jenna

Clues:

1. Jenna's team was not the smallest. They collected twice the percentage of paper as Neville's, but half the percentage of cans.
2. Yolanda and Charlie had the same number of helpers on their teams, but Yolanda's picked up four more pounds of trash than Charlie's.
3. Each person on Charlie's team picked up 23 pounds of trash.
4. There were six people on Neville's team, making it the largest.
5. Charlie's team picked up a total of 92 pounds of trash. Thirty-five percent of it was made up of bottles and other glass.
6. Jenna's team collected equal percentages of glass and paper and 15 percent cans.
7. Yolanda's team and Neville's team both picked up 24 pounds of glass. This is five percent more than the amount of paper Neville's team collected.
8. Charlie's team collected equal percentages of cans and plastic and 23 pounds of paper, ten pounds less paper than Jenna's team.
9. Yolanda's team collected an equal percentage of cans and plastic.
10. Neville's team collected 35 percent plastic. Yolanda's team collected an equal amount in paper.

Answer: Use the space below to work through the logic problem and write your answers.

_____

_____

_____

_____

_____

_____

_____

_____

_____

Solutions

Animal Friends (Page 1)
Ryan has a bird.
Angela has a cat.
Paul has a dog.
Anika has a fish.

Working Through the Clues:
1. Anika's pet does not have feathers.
   Anika does not have a bird.
2. Ryan's pet does not swim every day.
   Ryan does not have a fish.
3. The dog belongs to a boy.
   The dog belongs to Paul or Ryan.
   Neither Anika nor Angela has a dog.
4. Angela's pet has fur. The cat and dog have fur. The dog belongs to a boy, so Angela must have a cat.
5. Ryan's pet does not bark. Dogs bark, so Ryan does not have a dog. If Ryan does not have a cat (clue 4) or a fish (clue 2), then Ryan must have a bird. The dog belongs to a boy (clue 3), so Paul must have a dog. If Angela has a cat (clue 4), there is one student and one pet left. Anika must have a fish.

Summer Days (Page 2)
Top Row: Ethan, Hiroshi, Fernando
Bottom Row: Damon, Scott, Mark

Working Through the Clues:
1. The tallest boy has the lower bunk below the shortest boy.
2. Ethan is the youngest boy. He picked a top bunk on the left. Ethan is in top bunk #1.
3. Scott has the bunk below Hiroshi. Hiroshi has a top bunk and Scott has a lower bunk.
4. Fernando is the shortest boy.
   Fernando has an upper bunk (clue 1).
5. Damon has a bunk below the youngest boy. Damon is in lower bunk #1. Mark is the only boy left without a bunk, and the only bunk available is a lower.
6. Scott and Damon are not tall. Mark is the tallest boy. He has a lower bunk below Fernando (clues 1 and 4).
7. Hiroshi has a middle bunk to the right of the youngest boy. If Hiroshi has the upper bunk #2, then the order on the top is Ethan (clue 2), Hiroshi, and Fernando. The order in the lower bunks is Damon (clue 5), Scott, and Mark (clue 1).

And the Winner Is (Page 3)
Matthew: #2, fourth place
Vicente: #1, second place
Adara: #3, first place
Ashley: #4, third place

Working Through the Clues:
1. Matthew placed lower than Vicente. Matthew did not finish first.
2. The person in fourth place wore #2. Vicente did not wear #2.
3. The racer wearing #3 won. Matthew did not wear #3.
4. Ashley placed third. Ashley did not wear #3.
5. Vicente wore #1. Vicente did not win. He placed either second or fourth. If Matthew placed lower than Vicente (clue 1) then Matthew placed fourth and he wears #2 (clue 2). Vicente placed second. That means Adara won. She wore #3. Ashley wore #4.

Born In the U.S.A. (Page 4)
Jake was born in Florida.
Yanni was born in California.
Preston was born in Oklahoma.
Elise was born in New York.

Working Through the Clues:
1. Jake was not born in the Midwest. Jake was not born in Oklahoma.
2. Yanni was born in a coastal city. Yanni was not born in Oklahoma
3. Preston was born in a state west of where Jake was born. Preston was not born in New York or Florida.
4. Elise was not born in Florida.
5. Yanni traveled east to attend the reunion in Jake's state. If Yanni was born in a coastal city and traveled east to visit Jake, Yanni lives in California. If Preston lives west of Jake, but not in California, he must live in Oklahoma. If Elise was not born in Florida, then she was born in New York. Jake was born in Florida.

Zoo Art (Page 5)
Amanda drew a giraffe.
Kayla drew a zebra.
David drew an alligator.
Adam drew a flamingo.

Working Through the Clues:
1. Adam did not draw a mammal. Adam drew an alligator or a flamingo.
2. The animal David drew did not have stripes. David did not draw a zebra.
3. Amanda drew an animal that has a long neck, but no feathers. Amanda drew a giraffe.
4. David drew a picture of an animal with many sharp teeth. David drew a picture of an alligator, so Adam must have drawn a picture of a flamingo (clue 1). The only animal left is the zebra, so Kayla must have drawn the zebra.

At the Movies (Page 6)
Amy arrived at 1:20.
Jada arrived at 1:30.
Owen arrived at 1:50.
Nick arrived at 2:00.
Caleb arrived at 2:10.

Working Through the Clues:
1. The friends start their chores at noon, and the movie starts at 2:00 P.M.
2. Jada had four chores and each one took twenty minutes. It took ten minutes to get to the theater. Jada arrived at 1:30.
3. Caleb arrived later than Nick. Caleb did not arrive at 1:20.
4. Owen did not arrive first or last. Owen did not arrive at 1:20 or 2:10.
5. Amy arrived first. Amy arrived at 1:20.
6. Nick was not early or late. Nick arrived on time at 2:00. If Caleb arrived later than Nick, then he arrived late at 2:10. Owen must have arrived at 1:50

Whirlwind Tour (Page 7)
The order is England, France, Sweden, Germany, Italy.

Working Through the Clues:
1. They did not visit Germany first.
2. They visited Sweden before Italy but after France. So far, the order is France, Sweden, Italy.
3. They began their trip in a nation that recognizes English as the official language. They began their trip in England.
4. They took a train from England to France. Now the order is England, France, Sweden, Italy.
5. They visited Germany after Sweden but before Italy.

May I Take Your Coat? (Page 8)
Leah has #10.
Rachel has #21.
Karen has #23.
Maria has #24.

Working Through the Clues:
1. Maria and Leah both had red coats.
2. Karen's number was higher than Rachel's and lower than Maria's. At least two girls (Karen and Rachel) had numbers lower than Maria's, so Maria's number is 23 or 24.
3. The girl with #23 had a green coat. Maria had a red coat (clue #1) so her number must be 24. Leah also had a red coat so her number must be lower than 23.
4. Rachel had a blue coat. The girl with #23 had a green coat (clue 3) so Rachel cannot be #23. If Karen's number is higher than Rachel's (clue 2) and Leah is not #23 because she had a red coat (clue 3), then Karen is #23.
5. Leah and Maria had even numbers. There are two odd numbers and two even numbers. If Maria is #24 (clues 2 and 3), then Leah must have #10, so Rachel has #21.

Science Skills (Page 9)
Brody made a display about the life cycle of a moth.
Devin made a volcano model.
Michelle did a recycling project.
Sofia did a project with magnets.
Emilio did an experiment with plants and light.

Working Through the Clues:
1. Brody and the boy with black hair chose projects about living things. Brody's topic is either moths or plants.
2. The girl who works with magnets is Emilio's sister. Either Sofia or Michelle chose magnets as a topic.
3. Devin and his friend, who is doing the project on recycling, are blonde. Devin did not do the project on recycling. He is not working on a project about a living thing (clue 1). Emilio's topic is either moths or plants.
4. Michelle does not have a brother. Sofia is Emilio's sister and she is working with magnets (clue 2). If Devin is not doing recycling, moths, plants (clue 3), or magnets, he is making a volcano. That means that Michelle's topic is recycling.
5. Two of Brody's examples escaped from his project. Since plants don't escape, Brody must be working with moths. Emilio is working with plants.

Fun Fitness (Page 10)
Oscar won push-ups.
Cher won sit-ups.
Saul won the one-mile run.
Samantha won the one-hundred-yard dash.
Rodrigo won the rope climb.

Working Through the Clues:
1. Saul came in second in the one-hundred-yard dash and fourth in push-ups. Saul did not win the one-hundred-yard dash or push-ups.
2. A girl won sit-ups and placed second in push-ups. None of the boys won sit-ups.
3. Although they ran well, neither Rodrigo nor Cher won a race. Since he didn't win a race or sit-ups (clue 2) Rodrigo won either push-ups or rope climb.
4. The winner of the push-ups competition didn't enter any other events. Rodrigo entered several events so he must be the winner of the rope climb.
5. Samantha came in second in sit-ups. If Samantha came in second and a girl won (clue 2) then Cher must be the winner of sit-ups. If Saul did not win the one-hundred-yard dash or push-ups, he must be the winner of the one-mile run. If a girl placed second in the push-up competition (clue 2) a boy must have won it, so that would be Oscar. The only competition left is the one-hundred-yard dash, and the winner had to be Samantha.

Cake Walk (Page 11)
Alma sold cookies and made $100.
Rick sold cakes and made $55.
Susan sold cupcakes and made $80.
Pete sold pies and made $50.

Working Through the Clues:
1. Susan did not sell cakes, but she raised more money than the person who did.
2. Alma made twice as much money as the person who sold pies. Alma must have made $100. The person who sold pies made $50.
3. The person who sold cookies made more than $55. The person who sold cookies made either $80 or $100.
4. Pete made the least amount of money. Pete sold pies and made $50 (clue 2). If Alma made $100 and Susan made more than the person who sold cakes (clue 1) she must have made $80. That means that Rick must have sold cakes and made $55.
5. Alma's biggest sellers were ginger snaps and chocolate chip. Alma was selling cookies, so Susan must have sold cupcakes.

Dress Up (Page 12)
James was a pirate.
LeVar was a mummy.
Romy was a rock star.
Deanna was a mouse.
Paul was a chicken.

Working Through the Clues:
1. LeVar had decided to be a pirate, but changed his mind. LeVar was not a pirate.
2. Paul wore an animal costume. Paul was either a mouse or a chicken.
3. The girl who wore the rock star costume carried a toy guitar. None of the boys dressed as a rock star.
4. Deanna and the boy dressed as a pirate are cousins. Deanna was not dressed as a pirate.
5. The person dressed as a chicken and the girl dressed as a mouse applauded when LeVar won his prize. Levar did not dress as a mouse or a chicken. He did not dress as a pirate (clue 1) or a rock star (clue 3) so he must have worn the mummy costume. If a girl wore the mouse costume, then Paul must have dressed as a chicken (clue 2). If the person dressed as a pirate is a boy (clue 4), he must be James.
6. James' sister dressed as a rock star. If James and Deanna are cousins (clue 4), then Romy must be James' sister, and she dressed as a rock star. Deanna wore a mouse costume.

Right On Time (Page 13)
Swimming is scheduled at 9:00 A.M.
Canoeing is scheduled at 11:00 A.M.
Free time is scheduled at 1:00 P.M.
Hiking is scheduled at 3:00 P.M.
Crafts are scheduled at 4:00 P.M.

Working Through the Clues:
1. The campers have lunch at noon. They do something relaxing after lunch. Either crafts or free time must be scheduled for 1:00 P.M.
2. All lake activities are scheduled for before lunch. Swimming and canoeing take place in the morning.
3. Hiking is not the last activity of the day. If campers do something relaxing after lunch (clue 1), and hiking is not the last activity of the day, then they go hiking at 3:00 P.M.
4. The first activity of the day is Tom's favorite. His second favorite is canoeing. If Tom's favorite activity comes before canoeing, and swimming and canoeing are the morning activities (clue 2), then the first activity must be swimming at 9:00 A.M. Canoeing is scheduled for 11:00 A.M.
5. Tom usually chooses to nap or read a book at 1:00 P.M. If Tom is relaxing at 1:00 P.M., that must be the scheduled free time (clue 1). If hiking is scheduled for 3:00 P.M., then the campers must work on crafts at 4:00 P.M.

Weather Report (Page 14)
Monday was 63° and cloudy.
Tuesday was 59° with drizzle.
Wednesday was 57° with rain.
Thursday was 68° and partly cloudy.
Friday was 71° and sunny.

Working Through the Clues:
1. Wednesday was the coldest, wettest day of the week. It was two degrees colder than Tuesday. Wednesday was 57° with rain. Tuesday must have been 59°.
2. It did not rain or drizzle on Monday or Thursday.
3. Thursday was five degrees warmer than Monday. The only temperatures on Margo's list that are five degrees apart are 63° and 68°. Monday must have been 63°, and Thursday was 68°.
4. Margo needed her umbrella for two days in a row. If it did not rain or drizzle on Monday or Thursday, then the only two days in a row that could have had wet weather were Tuesday and Wednesday. If it rained on Wednesday, Tuesday must have had drizzle.
5. The wet weather was clearing on Thursday. Margo needed her sunglasses on Friday. If the weather was clearing, Thursday must have been partly cloudy. Friday was 71° and sunny. Monday must have been cloudy.

Pick a Card (Page 15)
Cody drew the queen.
Xavier drew the 7.
Owen drew the 4.
Matt drew the 2.
Antonio drew the ace.

Working Through the Clues:
1. Jack said that an ace would count as one and a picture card as ten.
2. Antonio did not draw a card with a number on it. Antonio drew either the ace or the queen.
3. Owen did not win, but his card was higher than Matt's and lower than Cody's.
4. Xavier rode before Antonio but after Cody. Xavier and Antonio must have drawn lower cards than Cody's. Antonio has the ace (clue 2). If Matt's and Owen's cards were also lower than Cody's (clue 3) then Cody must have drawn the queen.
5. Owen rode third. Cody rode first. Antonio rode fifth. Matt drew a lower card than Owen, so he must have ridden fourth. That means that Xavier rode second.

Class Favorites (Page 16)
Joshua's favorite subject is reading.
Grace's favorite subject is social studies.
Kyle's favorite subject is math.
Maria's favorite subject is science.
Tammy's favorite subject is art.

Working Through the Clues:
1. Maria's best friend loves art. Art is not Maria's favorite class.
2. Tammy's brother likes reading. Reading is not Tammy's favorite class. A boy likes reading.
3. Kyle does not enjoy social studies, and he does not have a sister. Joshua is Tammy's brother. His favorite class is reading.
4. Maria likes math and social studies, but they are not her favorites. Maria's favorite class is not math, social studies, art (clue 1), or reading (clues 2 and 3), so her favorite is science.
5. Tammy's best friend is Maria. Tammy's favorite subject is art (clue 1). If Kyle does not like social studies, then his favorite subject is math. Grace likes social studies.

Tournament Time (Page 17)
The Hot Shots finished first.
The Gold Rush finished second.
The Dragons finished third.
The Storm finished fourth.
The Tigers finished fifth.
The Razors finished sixth.
The Gators finished seventh.

Working Through the Clues:
1. The Gold Rush finished behind the Hot Shots and ahead of the Tigers and the Storm. The Gold Rush and the Hot Shots were not last or sixth. The Hot Shots were ahead of the Gold Rush.
2. The Razors and the Storm were not in last place.
3. The Tigers finished fifth ahead of the Razors. The Gold Rush and the Hot Shots placed fourth or higher. The Razors were not last (clue 2) so they finished sixth.
4. The Dragons finished higher than the Razors and the Storm but were not second or fourth. According to all the clues given, the Gators are in seventh place. If the Dragons are ahead of the Storm, the Razors are in sixth, the Tigers finished fifth (clue 3), and the Hot Shots and Gold Rush are ahead of the Storm, then the Storm finished fourth. If the Dragons did not finish second, they must have finished third. The Gold Rush was second, and the Hot Shots were first (clue 1).

Farm Fresh (Page 18)
Jim delivers lettuce second.
Angelo delivers onions fourth.
Tom delivers strawberries first.
Warren delivers tomatoes third.

Working Through the Clues:
1. Jim arrived at the market second, after the man who delivers strawberries. He did not deliver tomatoes. Jim does not deliver strawberries or tomatoes.
2. The man who delivers onions drives a black pickup truck. He arrived last. Jim does not drive a black pickup or deliver onions. He must deliver lettuce.
3. Warren, who drives a white van, used to deliver strawberries, but he changed jobs. Warren does not deliver strawberries or onions (clue 2), so he must deliver tomatoes.
4. Tom drives a blue van. He did not arrive third. If Tom did not arrive third, he must have arrived first (clues 1 and 2), so he delivers strawberries. Angelo must drive a black pickup and deliver onions.

A Friendly Game (Page 19)
Dylan chose handball.
Zeke chose dodgeball.
Rose chose soccer.
Zoe chose tetherball.
Sonny chose kickball.

Working Through the Clues:
1. Zeke is older than Sonny and Rose, who is not the youngest. Rose is younger than Zeke.
2. Dylan, who is wearing a red shirt, did not choose soccer or kickball.
3. The oldest student, a boy who is wearing a blue shirt, chose dodgeball. Dylan is wearing a red shirt, so he is not the oldest (clue 2). If Zeke is older than Sonny (clue 1), then Zeke is the oldest boy, and he chose dodgeball.
4. The youngest girl chose tetherball. If Rose is not the youngest girl (clue 1), then Zoe chose tetherball. If Dylan did not choose soccer or kickball (clue 2), he must have chosen handball.
5. A girl chose soccer. Rose chose soccer, and Sonny chose kickball.

Who's Next? (Page 20)
Amy is at 10:00 A.M.
Robert is at 11:00 A.M.
Chelsea is at 1:00 P.M.
Brook is at 2:00 P.M.
Benjamin is at 3:00 P.M.

Working Through the Clues
1. Chelsea's appointment is before Brook's and after 11:00 A.M.
2. A girl has the first appointment. Chelsea's appointment is after 11:00 (clue 1). If Brook's appointment is after Chelsea's, then she does not have the first appointment either. Amy has the 10:00 A.M. appointment.
3. Benjamin has an afternoon appointment. If Chelsea and Brook both have appointments after 11:00 A.M. (clue 1), and Benjamin's appointment is in the afternoon, then Robert must have the 11:00 A.M. appointment.
4. Brook does not have the last appointment. Benjamin must have the last appointment. Chelsea's is 1:00 P.M., and Brook's is 2:00 P.M.

Beach Day (Page 21)
There are 15 children in the youth group.
Sandwiches: 30
Drinks: 30
Cookies: 60
Beach Balls: 3
Beach Blankets: 5

Working Through the Clues:
1. They brought two sandwiches per person.
2. They brought half as many drinks as cookies. There were more cookies than drinks
3. They brought one beach ball for every five children. There were at least five children in the youth group.
4. They brought one beach blanket for every three children. If there were at least five children, then there were at least two blankets.
5. Each child had two drinks. If each child had two sandwiches, then the number of drinks and sandwiches were equal.
6. They brought 30 chocolate chip and 30 oatmeal cookies. There were 60 cookies altogether, so they brought 30 drinks (clues 2 and 5) and 30 sandwiches (clues 1 and 5). There must be 15 children (clue 1), three beach balls (clue 3), and five beach blankets (clue 4).

Summer Party (Page 22)
Number of guests: 7
Cost per guest: $10

Working Through the Clues:
1. Alejandro invited 25 percent of his class.
2. There were fewer than 30 students in Alejandro's class. Twenty-five percent of 30 is less than eight, so there were less than eight guests.

3. The refreshments were half the cost of the party.
4. The decorations cost 21 dollars. Twenty-one dollars is less than half the cost of the party.
5. Each guest received a party favor that cost two dollars.
6. The number of students in the class can be evenly divided by seven and 14. There were 28 students in Alejandro's class (clue 2). Alejandro invited seven guests (clue 1). The party favors cost 14 dollars (clue 5). If the decorations cost 21 dollars (clue 4), then the refreshments cost 35 dollars (clue 3). That means that the total cost was 70 dollars or ten dollars per guest.

Game Time (Page 23)
David: 20 points
Jacob: 12 points
Austin: 10 points
Sawyer: 6 points

Working Through the Clues:
1. The players earned two points for each basket.
2. David made more than three baskets. David made more than six points. He did not have the lowest score.
3. Austin scored more points than Sawyer. Austin did not have the lowest score.
4. Sawyer scored half as many points as Jacob. Jacob did not have the lowest score, so Sawyer must have made six points, and Jacob scored 12 points.
5. David scored twice as many points as Austin. David scored 20 points, and Austin scored ten points.

A Field Trip (Page 24)
Buses: 3
Total Round Trip: 50 miles
Time returned: 1:10 P.M.

Working Through the Clues:
1. The corner of Elm Avenue and Main Street is 11 miles from the museum.
2. Mrs. May's entire class rode on one bus, so there were twenty-seven students on one bus.
3. The class was at the museum for three hours.
4. The bus started on Grover Street, drove eight miles, and then went six miles on Main Street to Elm Avenue. The bus then went 11 more miles to the museum (clue 1). The trip to the museum was 25 miles, so the round trip was 50 miles.
5. The bus drove an average of 30 miles per hour. It took one hour and 40 minutes to make the round trip of 50 miles.

6. Four of Mrs. Corwin's students rode on the bus with Mr. Domenoske's class, so there were three buses with 27 students on each bus.
7. The class left for the museum at 8:30 A.M. The round trip took one hour and 40 minutes, and they visited the museum for three hours for a total time of four hours and 40 minutes. They returned to school at 1:10 P.M.

Gifts Galore (Page 25)
Patrick brought the candy.
Ruby brought the gift certificate.
Amanda brought the puzzle.
Nicole brought the CD.
Keenan brought the book.

Working Through the Clues
1. Ruby and the girl who brought the puzzle arrived early. Ruby did not bring the puzzle. A girl brought the puzzle, so that eliminates Keenan and Patrick.
2. The boy in the blue shirt brought candy. Keenan or Patrick brought the candy, so that eliminates Ruby, Amanda, and Nicole.
3. The girl who brought the CD had two pieces of cake. A girl brought the CD, so that eliminates Patrick and Keenan.
4. Amanda arrived with the girl who brought the gift certificate. Amanda did not bring the gift certificate. A girl brought the gift certificate, so that eliminates Keenan and Patrick.
5. Keenan is wearing a red shirt. A boy in a blue shirt brought candy (clue 2). Since Patrick is the only other boy, he must have brought the candy. Keenan did not bring the puzzle (clue 1), the CD (clue 3) or the gift certificate (clue 4). If Patrick brought the candy, then Keenan brought the book.
6. Amanda and Ruby did not eat cake. The girl who ate two pieces of cake brought the CD (clue 3), so Nicole must have brought the CD.
7. Keenan arrived with Nicole. If Nicole arrived with Keenan, then Ruby and Amanda arrived together, so Amanda brought the puzzle (clue 1), and Ruby brought the gift certificate (clue 4).

Weekend Work (Page 26)
North side of street: Mercados (feed fish)
　　　　　　　　　　　Shaws (Robin's last name)
　　　　　　　　　　　Carters (baby sit)
South side of street: Schumans (water plants)
　　　　　　　　　　　Trujillos (mow lawn)
　　　　　　　　　　　Feltons (walk dog)

Working Through the Clues

1. The Mercados live at the northwest end of the street.
2. Robin walked the dog for the people who lived directly south of the Carters. Robin did not walk the dog for the Mercados (clue 1) or the Carters. The Carters live on the same side of the street as the Mercados.
3. Robin feeds the fish for the family living west of the Shaws. Robin does not feed fish for the Shaws. The Shaws do not live on the west end of the street (Clue 1).
4. The Trujillos do not have a dog. Robin does not walk the dog for the Trujillos. The Trujillos do not live directly south of the Carters (clue 2).
5. Robin's family lives between the Mercados and the people who asked him to babysit. Robin's last name is not Mercado (clue 1). Robin must live on the north side of the street. Since the Carters live on the north side of the street (clue 2), Robin's family lives between the Carters and the Mercados. Robin babysits for the Carters.
6. Robin mows the lawn for the family living south of the Shaws. Robin does not mow the Shaws' or the Mercados' lawn (clue 1).
7. The Schumans live west of the Trujillos and south of the Mercados. The Trujillos must live between the Feltons on the east and the Schumans on the west. That means that Robin walks the dog for the Feltons (clue 2). He mows the lawn for the Trujiollos. The only name left is Shaw, so that must be Robin's last name. If he feeds the fish for the family who lives to the west of his (clue 3), then he does this job for the Mercados. The only job left is watering the plants, so that is what Robin does for the Schumans.

At the Fair (Page 27)
Aaron: yellow shirt, food service
Ann: red shirt, rides
Chloe: green shirt, petting zoo
Randy: blue shirt, games

Working Through the Clues

1. A girl is helping with rides. Ann or Chloe helps with rides.
2. Randy is wearing a blue shirt.
3. Aaron is not helping with games. Aaron helps with food or the petting zoo, but not rides (clue 1) or games.
4. Chloe does not have a yellow shirt. Chloe has a red or green shirt, but not blue (clue 2) or yellow.

5. Ann is wearing a red shirt. If Ann is wearing a red shirt, then Chloe is wearing green (clue 4). If Ann is wearing red, Chloe is wearing green, and Randy is wearing blue (clue 2), then Aaron is wearing yellow.
6. The girl helping with the petting zoo is not wearing red. Chloe is wearing green, so she helps with the petting zoo. If a girl helps with rides (clue 1), it must be Ann.
7. The boy wearing yellow is helping with food. Aaron is helping with food (clue 6), so Randy is helping with games.

Family Matters (Page 28)
Grady, Austin, and Kelsey are related.
Tyler, Brandon, and Haley are related.
Daniel, Ana, and Nathan are related.
Anthony, Carlos, and Marissa are related.

Working Through the Clues

1. Tyler's sister and Kelsey are in the same class. They are best friends. Kelsey is not Tyler's sister.
2. Haley's brother is three years older than she is. He is a soccer goalie on the eighth-grade team. Haley is in fifth grade.
3. Grady's brother, Austin, is in high school. He is in the same grade as Daniel's brother. Austin is Grady's brother.
4. Brandon is in eighth grade. Brandon is not Daniel's brother (clue 3).
5. Carlos is a forward on the same soccer team as Haley's brother. His sister is sixteen. Since his sister is sixteen and Haley is in fifth grade, Carlos is not Haley's brother. Brandon is Haley's brother (clue 2). Carlos is in eighth grade (clues 2 and 4), so he is not Daniel's brother (clue 3). If Carlos' sister is sixteen, Kelsey cannot be his sister (clue 2).
6. Haley often goes to the movies with her best friend, Kelsey. Hayley is Tyler's sister (clue 1), and Brandon is Tyler's brother (5). If Brandon is Tyler's brother, Austin is Grady's brother (clue 3), and Carlos is not Daniel's brother (clue 5), Carlos must be Anthony's brother.
7. Ana is three years old. Carlos' sister is sixteen (clue 5). Ana cannot be his sister, so his sister is Marissa.
8. Nathan is in high school. Nathan is Daniel's brother (clue 3).
9. Sometimes Kelsey babysits for Daniel's little sister. If Kelsey is not Daniel's sister, she must be Grady's sister. Ana is three years old (clue 7), so she must be Daniel's sister.

The Play Is the Thing (Page 29)
William plays the musician.
Alexander plays the mayor.
Emma plays the toy soldier.
Mary plays the cook.
Christopher plays the toymaker.

Working Through the Clues
1. Mr. Jagellio chose the shortest student to play the mayor.
2. Neither Mary nor Emma can play an instrument, so neither could be the musician. A boy plays the musician.
3. The students who play the toymaker and the cook are brother and sister.
4. Mary does not play the mayor. Mary is not the shortest student (clue 1).
5. William does not have a sister. William is not the toymaker or the cook (clue 3).
6. A blonde girl has the part of the toy soldier. Either Emma or Mary plays the toy soldier.
7. Christopher and William are both tall. They do not play the mayor (clue 1). If William does not play the mayor, the toymaker, the cook (clues 3 and 5), or the toy soldier (clue 6), then he is the musician.
8. The student who plays the toymaker plays piano.
9. Alexander is an only child. Alexander does not play the part of the toymaker or the cook (clue 3). If he does not play toy soldier (clue 6), then he plays the mayor.
10. Mary has brown hair. Mary does not play the part of the toy soldier (clue 6). Emma must play the toy soldier. Mary must be the cook because she cannot play a musical instrument (clue 2), and the student who is the toymaker plays piano (clue 8). Mary's brother, Christopher, is the toymaker.

On the Field (Page 30)
Lucas is the goalie.
Sean is the sweeper.
Joe is the left wing.
Ian is the forward.
Mark is the fullback.

Working Through the Clues
1. Sean is not a forward. His best friend is the left wing. Sean is not the left wing.
2. The youngest boy lives on the third floor, two floors above Lucas. Lucas lives on the first floor.
3. The sweeper's best friend is Joe. Joe is not the sweeper.
4. The goalie and Mark are best friends. Mark is not the goalie.

5. The forward lives on the third floor. Sean does not live on the third floor (clue 1). The forward is the youngest player (clue 2).
6. The boy who lives on the first floor is the goalie. Lucas is the goalie (clue 2). His best friend is Mark (clue 4).
7. Ian is the youngest. His best friend does not play soccer. Ian is the forward (clues 2 and 5). If Ian's best friend is not on the team, and Lucas and Mark are best friends (clue 6), then Sean and Joe must be best friends. Sean's best friend is the left wing (clue 1), so Joe is the left wing and Sean is the sweeper (clue 3). The only position left is fullback, so Mark must be the fullback.

Practice Makes Perfect (Page 31)
They rode 1.5 miles on Willow first.
They rode 3 miles on Brookside second.
They rode 4 miles on Atlanta third.
They rode 3.5 miles on Regent fourth.
They rode 2 miles on Pine fifth.

Working Through the Clues
1. They rode further on Brookside than on Pine.
2. They rode further on Atlanta than Regent.
3. Priscilla chose to do the shortest stretch first, then turn onto Brookside. Brookside is longer than 1.5 miles.
4. They rode the 4-mile stretch before the 3.5-mile stretch.
5. They rode the last 2 miles on Pine.
6. They rode further on Regent than on Brookside. By comparing this information with the information in clues 1 and 2, the order from shortest to longest stretch is Pine, Brookside, Regent, and Atlanta. If the length of the Pine stretch is 2 miles (clue 5), the 1.5-mile stretch is Willow. They rode Willow first, Brookside second (clue 3), Atlanta, then Regent (clue 4), and Pine last (clue 5).

Summer Reading (Page 32)
Meena read *Spring, The Mystery of King Lake, Stormy*, and *The First Robin*.
José read *The Funny Guy, Later That Day, The Fear Speaker,* and *Hill Street*.

Working Through the Clues
1. Meena likes mysteries. Meena read *The Mystery of King Lake* and *Stormy*.
2. The title of the fourth book he read reminded José of his school.
3. Meena enjoys humor, but she didn't read a humorous book. José read *The Funny Guy*.

4. José did not read a book with a one-word title. Meena read *Spring* and *Stormy*.

5. Meena saved her nonfiction book for last. Meena read *The First Robin* fourth. José read *The Fear Speaker, Later That Day,* and *Hill Street.*

6. José and Meena attend the Hill Street School. José read *Hill Street* last (clue 2).

7. Meena read the fantasy before she read *The Mystery of King Lake.*

8. José did not start with a scary book. He read *The Fear Speaker* after the scary book. José read *The Funny Guy* first (clue 3), *Later That Day* second, and *The Fear Speaker* third.

9. Meena read *Stormy* third. Meena read *Spring* first and *The Mystery of King Lake* second (clue 7). She read *Stormy* third and *The First Robin* last (clue 5).

Spooky Tales (Page 33)

Nina told about a werewolf in a shopping mall.
Andrew told about a vampire in an old house.
Noah told about a zombie in an empty school.
Emily told about a mummy in a cemetery.
Nicolas told about a ghost in a swamp.

Working Through the Clues

1. Noah pictured his character in a darkened classroom. Noah's setting is an empty school.

2. The ghost story is not set in an old building or a cemetery. The ghost is not in an old school or house. It is in a swamp or shopping mall. Noah did not tell the ghost story (clue 1).

3. Nicolas wanted to do a vampire story, but he changed his mind. Nicolas did not tell about a vampire.

4. Nina's character doesn't drink blood, but it does have sharp teeth and fur. Nina's character is a werewolf.

5. Emily set her story in an outdoor place, but not a swamp. Emily's story is set in a cemetery.

6. Andrew did not tell about a zombie or a mummy. If Nina's character is a werewolf (clue 4), then Andrew wrote about a vampire or a ghost.

7. A girl told the mummy story. If Nina's character is a werewolf (clue 4), then Emily told the mummy story.

8. Nina and Andrew did not use an outdoor setting. Emily's story is in a cemetery (clue 5), so Nicolas told a story set in a swamp.

9. The werewolf story was not set in an old house. The only setting left is a shopping mall, so Nina told a story about a werewolf in a shopping mall. That means the ghost story is set in a swamp (clue 2), so Nicolas told about a ghost in a swamp. The only

setting left is an old house. If Andrew did not tell about a zombie (clue 6), then he told about a vampire in an old house. That means Noah told about a zombie in an empty school (clue 1).

Perfect Pizza (Page 34)

Marcus and Harry shared a pizza with onions and sausage.
Dimitri and Tai shared a pizza with mushrooms and peppers.
Melanie and Holly shared a pizza with double cheese and pepperoni.

Working Through the Clues

1. Tai does not eat meat. She does not want pepperoni or sausage.

2. Holly will not eat peppers.

3. Pizza #1 combines double cheese and pepperoni. Tai does not share pizza #1.

4. Dimitri loves mushrooms. He doesn't mind peppers, but he would prefer not to have onions.

5. Two people like sausage. One of them shared a pizza with Marcus.

6. Melanie likes sausage and pepperoni.

7. Pizza #2 combines mushrooms and peppers. Holly did not share pizza #2 (clue 2). The only toppings left are sausage and onions on pizza #3. Tai will not eat meat (clue 1), so she must have shared pizza #2. Marcus shared pizza #3 (clue 5).

8. Melanie does not like onions or mushrooms. Marcus likes onions a lot and Harry doesn't mind them. Melanie won't eat onions, so Marcus and Harry share pizza #3. Dimitri loves mushrooms (clue 4) and he doesn't mind peppers, so he shares pizza #2 with Tai. Melanie shares pizza #1 with Holly (clue 6 and 8).

New Friends (Page 35)

The Coffman family adopted Blue the dog.
The Stein family adopted Woodrow the cat.
The Rodriguez family adopted Tucker the dog.
The Rogers family adopted Max the cat.
The Shindri family adopted Angel the cat.
The Wolf family adopted Mischief the dog.

Working Through the Clues

1. Angel is the only female cat.

2. The Wolf family adopted a dog, but not Blue, the male Chihuahua. Blue is a dog.

3. The Rogers family already has a dog but no cat. They adopted a male cat. The Rogers family did not adopt Angel.

4. Tucker is young black labrador. Tucker is a large dog.

66

5. A family with two cats adopted Woodrow. The Rogers family did not adopt Woodrow (clue 2).

6. Mischief is an older coonhound. If Mischief, Blue (clue 2), and Tucker (clue 4) are dogs, then Woodrow and Max are cats.

5. The Coffmans adopted a small male dog. The Coffmans adopted Blue (clue 2).

7. The Shindris do not have any pets. The Shindris did not adopt Woodrow (clue 5).

8. The Rogers family did not adopt a dog, but the Rodriguez family did. The Shindris and the Steins adopted cats. If the Rogers and Shindris did not adopt Woodrow (clues 2, 5, and 7), then the Steins adopted Woodrow. If the Rogers adopted a male cat (clue 2), then they adopted Max, and the Shindris adopted Angel.

9. The Wolf family adopted an older pet. The Wolf family adopted Mischief (clue 6), so the Rodriguez family adopted Tucker.

Gift Exchange (Page 36)

Venisha gave bubble bath to Nancy.
Isabel gave lip gloss to Venisha.
Reba gave a book to Lonnie.
Nancy gave hair clips to Isabel.
Lonnie gave chocolates to Reba.

Working Through the Clues

1. Lonnie drew the name of the youngest girl. Lonnie is not the youngest girl.

2. Venisha did not receive an edible gift. Venisha did not receive chocolates.

3. Isabel is younger than Nancy and older than Reba. Reba is younger than Isabel and Nancy. Lonnie did not draw Nancy or Isabel (clue 1). She drew Venisha or Reba.

4. Nancy did not draw Venisha's name.

5. Isabel gave lip gloss to the oldest girl. Isabel did not give a gift to Reba.

6. Lonnie received a book from the girl to whom she gave a gift. Neither Nancy nor Isabel exchanged gifts with Lonnie. Nor did Nancy or Isabel receive a book (clues 1 and 3).

7. Venisha, who is older than Lonnie, gave bubble bath.

8. Lonnie gave an edible gift. Lonnie gave chocolates. Venisha did not receive chocolates (clue 2), so Lonnie drew Reba (clue 3). That means that Reba is the youngest girl (clue 1). She drew Lonnie and gave her a book (clue 6).

9. Nancy is not the oldest girl. The oldest girl is Venisha. She received lip gloss from Isabel. If Isabel drew Venisha (clue 5), and Lonnie and Reba exchanged gifts (clues 6 and 8), then Nancy drew

Isabel's name, and Venisha drew Nancy's. Venisha gave bubble bath to Nancy (clue 7). That leaves hair clips, which Nancy gave to Isabel.

Good Morning (Page 37)

Michael had pancakes with maple syrup and milk.
Taryn had eggs and toast with tea.
Lizbeth had waffles with strawberry syrup and orange juice.
Mom had cereal and coffee.
Dad had an omelet and tomato juice.

Working Through the Clues

1. Dad had an egg dish, but Michael did not.

2. Mom did not have syrup. Mom did not eat pancakes or waffles.

3. Michael did not drink juice or coffee. Michael had tea or milk.

4. The person who had the omelet drank tomato juice.

5. Mom did not have a hot breakfast, but she did have a hot drink. Mom had cereal with coffee or tea.

6. Lizbeth does not like maple syrup. Lizbeth did not have pancakes.

7. The person who had eggs and toast drank tea. Mom had coffee with her cereal (clue 5). Michael did not have tea, so he drank milk (clues 1 and 3).

8. Dad had juice. If Dad had juice, then he had an omelet with tomato juice (clues 1, 4, and 7).

9. Lizbeth did not have milk or tea. Lizbeth must have had orange juice. That means she did not have eggs and toast (clue 7). She did not have pancakes (clue 6), so she had waffles. Michael did not have eggs, so he must have had pancakes and milk (clues 1 and 7). Taryn had eggs and toast with tea.

Pick a Number (Page 38)

Luke picked #12.
Riley picked #33.
Adam picked #45.
Cameron picked # 22.
Lucia picked #17.
Mrs. Arnold picked #30.
Riley took the hamster home for the weekend.

Working Through the Clues

1. Luke's number could not be divided by ten or 11. Luke did not pick 22, 30 or 33.

2. Mrs. Arnold picked an even number. She did not pick 33, 17, or 45.

3. Adam's number could be divided by five. Adam picked 30 or 45.

4. Luke's number was lower than Adam's. Luke picked 12, 17, or 45 (clue 1). Luke's number is lower than Adam's, so Luke picked 12 or 17.

5. Riley's number was higher than Mrs. Arnold's number.

6. Lucia and Adam picked odd numbers. They picked 17, 33, or 45. If Adam's number can be divided by 5 (clue 3), then he must have picked 45.

7. Cameron has a lower number than Mrs. Arnold.

8. Riley's number could be divided by three but not ten. Riley chose 33. That means Lucia picked 17, so Luke picked 12 (clue 4). If Cameron's number was lower than Mrs. Arnold's (clue 7), Cameron picked 22, which leaves 30 for Mrs. Arnold. Riley got to take the hamster home.

On Stage (Page 39)

On Monday, 35 afternoon and 75 evening tickets were sold.

On Tuesday, 55 afternoon and 100 evening tickets were sold.

On Wednesday, 45 afternoon and 30 evening tickets were sold.

On Thursday, 20 afternoon and 40 evening tickets were sold.

Working Through the Clues

1. Wednesday was the only day when students sold more afternoon than evening tickets.

2. The highest number of afternoon tickets were sold on Tuesday.

3. Fewer evening tickets were sold on Wednesday than Thursday.

4. On Thursday, sales for afternoon tickets were exactly half those of evening tickets. The only pair of numbers that fits this clue are 20 and 40. On Thursday, students sold 20 afternoon and 40 evening tickets.

5. The highest ticket sales for any performance were on Tuesday. Students sold 100 tickets for the evening performance on Tuesday.

6. Ten more tickets were sold for the afternoon performance on Wednesday than on Monday.

7. The second-highest ticket sales for any performance were sold on Monday. More evening than afternoon tickets were sold on Monday (clue 1). The second-highest sales amount is 75, so that's how many evening tickets were sold on Monday.

8. Students sold 35 afternoon tickets on Monday. If 35 afternoon tickets were sold on Monday, then 45 were sold on Wednesday (clue 6). If fewer evening than afternoon tickets were sold on Wednesday (clue 1), then 30 evening tickets were sold. That leaves 55 afternoon tickets sold on Tuesday.

In the Bank (Page 40)

There is $10.03 in the green puppy bank for a rainy day.

There is $3.17 in the yellow pig bank for candy.

There is $14.22 in the pink bunny bank for a gift for Mom.

There is $5.74 in the blue kitten bank to get a pet rat.

Working Through the Clues

1. There is more in the blue bank than the yellow bank and less in the blue bank then the green bank. The order from lowest amount of money to highest is yellow, blue, green.

2. Anisa saved more money for a rainy day than for candy.

3. The money for her pet rat is in the kitten bank.

4. There is $10.03 in the green puppy bank. If there is more money in the green bank than the blue and yellow banks, the largest amount, $14.22, must be in the pink bank. There must be $3.17 in the yellow bank and $5.74 in the blue bank.

5. She keeps her candy money in her pig bank. The pig bank is not green (clue 4) so she has not saved $10.03 for candy.

6. The bunny bank holds the most money. The bunny bank must be pink. She has not saved $14.22 for her rat (clue 3) or candy (clue 5).

7. Her kitten bank is blue. The kitten bank holds $5.74 (clues 3 and 4) for her pet rat.

8. The money for her Mom's gift is not in the green bank. Nor is it in the blue bank (clue 7).

9. The pig bank is not pink. It is not green (clue 4) or blue (clue 7), so the pig bank is yellow. Anisa has saved $3.17 for candy. The money for her Mom's gift must be in the pink bunny bank, and her money for a rainy day must be in the green puppy bank.

The Winning Ticket (Page 41)

Mr. Bates bought 1 ticket and won a plant.

Ms. Amos bought 5 tickets and won a stuffed bear.

Mr. Hunter bought 6 tickets and won a blender.

Mr. Perch bought 10 tickets and won roller blades.

Mrs. Heinz bought 3 tickets and won movie tickets.

Working Through the Clues

1. The person who bought 10 tickets won roller blades.

2. Mr. Hunter bought more tickets than Ms. Amos. Ms. Amos did not win roller blades.

3. Mr. Bates did not win movie tickets.

4. The person who won the blender bought more tickets than Mr. Bates. Mr. Bates did not win a blender or roller blades (clue 1).

5. Mrs. Heinz bought fewer tickets than the woman who won the bear, but more than Mr. Bates. A man did not win the bear. Mrs. Heinz did not win the bear, so Ms. Amos won the bear. Mrs. Heinz bought fewer tickets than Mr. Hunter (clue 2).

6. Mr. Bates did not buy 10 tickets. Mr. Bates did not win roller blades, movie tickets (clue 3), a blender (clue 4), or the bear (clue 5), so he won a plant.

7. Mr. Perch could not put his prize in his pocket. Mr. Perch did not win movie tickets.

8. The man who won the blender gave it to his mother. Mrs. Heinz did not win the blender.

9. Mr. Hunter did not buy the most or the least tickets. Mr. Hunter did not win roller blades (clue 1). Mrs. Heinz did not buy ten tickets (clues 2 and 5). Mr. Perch won the roller blades. A man won the blender (clue 8), so Mrs. Heinz won movie tickets, and Mr. Hunter won the blender. Mr. Hunter bought more tickets than Mr. Bates (clue 4) and more tickets than Ms. Amos (clue 2). Mrs. Heinz bought fewer tickets than Ms. Amos but more than Mr. Bates (clue 5), so the order is Mr. Bates 1 ticket, Mrs. Heinz 3 tickets, Ms. Amos 5 tickets, and Mr. Hunter 6 tickets.

Spelling Bee (Page 42)

Alisha was first and misspelled *asteroid*.
Arthur was second and misspelled *psychology*.
Briana was third and misspelled *gadget*.
Collin was fourth and won by spelling *correspond*.
Tom was fifth and misspelled *barnacle*.

Working Through the Clues

1. Alisha, who was first in line, misspelled an eight-letter word. Alisha did not win. Her word was either *asteroid* or *barnacle*.

2. The girl who was third in line misspelled *gadget*. A boy won. *Gadget* was not the winning word. Alisha misspelled an eight-letter word (clue 1), so Briana was third in line and lost when she misspelled *gadget*.

3. Tom did not spell his word correctly.

4. Collin was not second in line. He was either fourth or fifth (clue 2).

5. The fourth student in line was the winner.

6. Arthur misspelled a ten-letter word. Arthur did not win. He was not first, third, or fourth in line (clue 3 and 5). He misspelled either *psychology* or *correspond*.

7. The boy who was fifth in line misspelled the word *barnacle*. Arthur was not fifth (clue 6), so he was second. *Barnacle* was not the winning word. Alisha misspelled *asteroid* (clue 1). If Collin was not fifth in line (clue 4), Tom was fifth, and he misspelled the word *barnacle*. Collin must be the winner.

8. Collin's word was not last alphabetically. Collin's word was not *psychology*, so it must be *correspond*.

Snack Attack (Page 43)

Zoey spent $10: ticket ($5), nachos ($3), juice ($2)
Haley spent $8: ticket ($5), candy ($2), water ($1)
Rose spent $6: ticket ($3), popcorn ($1), soda ($2)

Working Through the Clues:

1. Zoey spent the most money.

2. Rose had a two-dollar discount coupon for her ticket, so she spent three dollars for her ticket (clue 2 and 5).

3. The candy cost two-thirds as much as nachos and twice as much as popcorn. Popcorn was the least expensive snack, and nachos were the most expensive.

4. The girl who had water did not spend the least.

5. The final total for the tickets was thirteen dollars. Rose had a $2 coupon, so the full price was $15. Rose's ticket was three dollars, and the others were five dollars.

6. The girl who bought nachos also bought juice.

7. Soda and juice cost the same as candy and twice as much as water. Water was the least expensive drink.

8. The least expensive snack cost one dollar. Popcorn cost one dollar. Candy cost two dollars, and nachos three dollars (clue 3). Soda and juice cost two dollars, and water cost one dollar (clue 7). The most expensive snack and drink combination is nachos and juice at five dollars. Since Zoey spent the most money (clue 1), she paid five dollars for her ticket and bought nachos and juice for five dollars (clue 6).

9. Rose's snack cost half as much as her drink. Rose had popcorn and soda for three dollars (clues 7 and 9). If her ticket cost three dollars, then she spent six dollars, the least amount. That means that Haley had candy and water for three dollars. If her ticket cost five dollars, then she spent a total of eight dollars (clue 4).

Teaming Up (Page 44)

There are thirty students in the class.
Ruth's team: 4 boys and 6 girls
Nelson's team: 5 boys and 5 girls
José's team: 7 boys and 3 girls

Working Through the Clues:

1. There are fewer than 40 students in the class.

2. Half the class, less one, are girls. There are two more boys than girls in the class.

3. One-quarter of the boys are on Ruth's team. There are fewer than five boys on her team.

4. There are an equal number of students on each team. The number of students in the class can be divided equally by three.

5. There are an odd number of girls on Nelson and José's teams.

6. The total number of students can be divided by two, three, five, ten, and fifteen. Since there are fewer than 40 students in the class (clue 1), the number of students must be 30. That means that there are 14 girls and 16 boys (clue 2). Four boys are on Ruth's team (clue 3), so six girls are on Ruth's team.

7. There are four fewer girls than boys on José's team. If there are ten students on each team (clue 4), and there are six girls on Ruth's team (clue 3), there are a total of eight girls on the other two teams (clue 2). If there are an odd number of girls on José's team (clue 5), and there are four less girls than boys on José's team, then the number of girls on José's team is one or three.

8. The number of boys and girls on Nelson's team is equal. If there are ten students on Nelson's team (clue 4), then there must be five girls and five boys. That leaves three girls on José's team and seven boys.

Shopping Spree (Page 45)
Emma: Brought $21.00, Allowance $10.50, Balance $1.00
Megan: Brought $30.00, Allowance $10.00, Balance $15.00
Latoya: Brought $48.00, Allowance $12.00, Balance $18.00

Working Through the Clues:
1. Emma had saved two weeks' allowance for the shopping trip. Emma had at least $20.

2. Megan only bought a sweater that was 50% off the original price of $30. Megan spent $15.

3. Latoya receives a greater allowance than Emma. Emma does not get $12 per week.

4. Megan saved half of her allowance for six weeks for the shopping trip. Megan brought an amount equal to three weeks of allowance. She had at least $30.

5. Emma spent $12.00 on a gift for her mother. She bought a hair band for $3.00 and a belt for $5.00. Emma spent $20.00.

6. Latoya spent one-fourth of her money on a wallet. Then she spent half of what she had left on a pair of shoes.

7. Emma had a balance of $1.00. If Emma spent $20.00 (clue 5) and she has $1.00 left, then she started with $21.00. Since this was two weeks' allowance (clue 1) then her allowance is $10.50.

Latoya's allowance is $12.00 (clue 3). Megan's allowance is $10.00, so she brought $30.00 (clue 4). Megan spent $15.00 (clue 2) so her balance was $15.00.

8. Latoya had $3.00 more than Megan when they left the mall. If Megan had $15.00, then Latoya had a balance of $18.00. That means she spent $18.00 on a pair of shoes (clue 6). Latoya had $36 left after her first purchase. That amount represented 3/4 of the total she started with, so she started with $48.00.

A Pack of Puppies (Page 46)
Shiloh: 5 pounds, adopted by the Coopers
Chelsea: 6 pounds, adopted by the Guerreros
Tramp: 8 pounds, adopted by the Capaldis
Stitch: 7 $\frac{1}{2}$ pounds, adopted by the Sullivans
Chatelet: 5 $\frac{1}{2}$ pounds, adopted by the Coopers

Working Through the Clues:
1. There are three female and two male puppies.

2. The Coopers adopted two female puppies.

3. Shiloh is the smallest puppy. Shiloh weighs 5 pounds.

4. Stitch and Tramp are both males. The Coopers did not adopt Stitch or Tramp

5. The Guerreros adopted Chelsea. Chelsea is a female. The Coopers adopted Shiloh and Chatelet (clue 2).

6. The Capaldis adopted the largest puppy. Their puppy weighs 8 pounds. The Capaldis puppy must be a male, so they adopted either Tramp or Stitch.

7. Chatelet weighs two pounds less than Stitch. Chatelet weighs either 5 $\frac{1}{2}$ or 6 pounds.

8. The Sullivans' puppy weighs 1 $\frac{1}{2}$ pounds more than Chelsea. The only 1 $\frac{1}{2}$ pound difference is between 6 pounds and 7 $\frac{1}{2}$ pounds. Chelsea must weigh 6 pounds. That means that Chatelet weighs 5 $\frac{1}{2}$ pounds and Stitch weighs 7 $\frac{1}{2}$ pounds (clue 7). Stitch was adopted by the Sullivans. Tramp was adopted by the Capaldis and weighs 8 pounds (clue 6).

Travis' Bookcase (Page 47)
Nonfiction: shelf #1 has 6 books
Adventure: shelf #2 has 12 books
Mysteries: shelf #3 has 6 books
Mysteries: shelf #4 has 8 books
Biographies: shelf #5 has 10 books

Working Through the Clues
1. One-third of the books are mysteries.
2. There are twice as many books on the second from the top as on shelf #3.

3. The adventure books are on a shelf above the biographies. The adventure books are not on shelf #5 because #5 is the lowest shelf. There must be at least one shelf below the adventure books for biographies.

4. There are the same number of books on the top shelf and the third shelf.

5. There are a total of 42 books. Fourteen books are mysteries (clue 1).

6. The mysteries are on two shelves, one directly above the other.

7. There are no books above nonfiction. Nonfiction is on shelf #1, so mystery, adventure, and biography are below shelf #1. Because nonfiction is on shelf #1, mysteries cannot be a combination of shelves #1 and #2 (clue 6).

8. There are six books on shelf #3. If there are six books on shelf #3, there are six books on shelf #1 (clue 4). There are twelve books on shelf #2 (clue 2). Mysteries cannot be on a combination of shelves #2 and #3 because there are sixteen books on those two shelves combined. There are only fourteen mysteries (clue 5).

9. Biographies are on a shelf below the mysteries. If biographies are on a shelf below them, the mysteries cannot be on shelves #4 and #5. The mysteries must be on shelves #3 and #4. If nonfiction is on shelf #1 (clue 7), mysteries are on shelves #3 and #4, and adventure books are above biographies (clue 3), then adventure must be on shelf #2, and biography is on shelf #5. There are fourteen mysteries altogether (clue 5). If there are six books on shelf #3, there must be eight books on shelf #2. There are six books on shelf #1 (clues 4 and 8), eight books on shelf #2, six books on shelf #3 (clue 8), and twelve books on shelf #4 (clues 2 and 8) for a total of thirty-two books. If there are 42 books altogether (clue 5), that leaves a balance of ten books on shelf #5.

Running for Office (Page 48)

Tanya Baggins is vice president.
Alexis Wilson is treasurer.
Bud Thomas is secretary.
Craig Harlow is president.

Working Through the Clues
1. The only student elected who plays soccer is the secretary.
2. The president's last name is Harlow.
3. The vice president is a girl. Neither Bud nor Craig is vice president.
4. Tanya's last name is Baggins. Tanya is not president (clue 2).
5. The student whose favorite hobby is robotics does not live next door to another student.

6. Craig is not on a sports team. Craig is not secretary (clue #1).

7. The person with the last name of Thomas lives next door to the treasurer. Tanya does not live next door to the treasurer (clue 4).

8. Alexis Wilson's favorite hobby is photography. Alexis is not president (clue 2). She does not live next door to the treasurer (clue 7).

9. Craig does not live next door to another student. Craig does not live next door to the treasurer, so his last name is not Thomas (clue 7). If Tanya and Alexis do not live next door to the treasurer (clues 4 and 7), then Bud does, and his last name is Thomas. If Bud's name is Thomas, Tanya's is Baggins, and Alexis' is Wilson, then Craig's name is Harlow, and he is president. If Bud is not president, vice president (clue 3), or treasurer (clue 7), then he is secretary.

10. Craig's favorite hobby is rock collecting. Craig does not live next door to another student (clue 9). The person whose favorite hobby is robotics does not live next door to another student (clue 5). Since Craig's favorite hobby is rock collecting and Alexis's favorite hobby is photography (clue 8), and Bud lives next door to the treasurer, Tanya must be the robotics enthusiast. That means that Alexis lives next door to another student. She must live next to Bud, which means she is the treasurer, and Tanya is the vice president.

Author Author (Page 49)

Ahmed, age 11, won first place for "Smooth Hands."
Bethany, age 12, won second place for "Pig Sty."
Joshua, age 14, won third place for "Gone."
Gina, age 10, won fourth place for "The Top of the World."

Working Through the Clues
1. Joshua is two years older than the person who came in second. Joshua is 12 or 14. The person who came in second is either 10 or 12.
2. Bethany is two years older than the person who placed fourth. Bethany is either 12 or 14. The person who placed fourth is either 10 or 12.
3. "Gone" didn't win first or second place.
4. Ahmed was neither the youngest nor the oldest writer. Ahmed is either 11 or 12.
5. "The Top of the World" was the only nonfiction entry, and it was by the youngest writer.
6. The person who came first was not Gina.
7. "Pig Sty" won a higher place than "The Top of the World" but lower than "Smooth Hands." "Pig Sty" and "The Top of the World" did not win first place.
8. Ahmed placed higher than Bethany.

9. Joshua placed higher than the youngest writer, but lower than the 11-year-old. Joshua did not take first place. If Gina nor Bethany came in first (clues 6 and 8), then Ahmed won first place.

10. The story "Smooth Hands" placed higher than "Gone" and "The Top of the World." If "Smooth Hands" and "Gone" placed higher than "The Top of the World," and "Pig Sty" placed higher than "The Top of the World" (clue 7), then "The Top of the World" came in fourth. The writer is age 10 (clue 5). That means that Bethany is 12 (clue 2), and Joshua is 14 (clue 1). In addition, if Bethany is two years younger than Joshua, she won second place (clue 1). Ahmed won first place (clue 9), so the only place left is third. Joshua must have won third. If "Gone" didn't win first or second place (clue 3), and it didn't come in last, it must have come in third, so Joshua wrote "Gone." If Gina did not come in first (Ahmed), second (Bethany), or third (Joshua), then she came in fourth and wrote "The Top of the World." "Smooth Hands" placed higher than "Pig Sty" (clue 7), so it came in first.

Picture Perfect (Page 50)

The watercolor farm scene is in the den in a green frame.

The bowl of apples in oils is in the kitchen in a red frame.

The watercolor lake scene is in the living room in a blue frame.

The self-portrait in oils is in the dining room in a brown frame.

Working Through the Clues

1. Two of the paintings were done in watercolor. Two of the paintings were done with oils.

2. The watercolor painting in the den has a green frame.

3. The painting with the brown frame is in the dining room.

4. The painting in the dining room was not done in watercolor. The painting in the dining room was done in oils.

5. Jenna's favorite painting is in a red frame. Her favorite painting is not in the den.

6. Jenna painted the self-portrait in oils. The self-portrait is not in the den. It does not have a green frame.

7. The bowl of apples is Jenna's favorite painting. The bowl of apples is in a red frame (clue 5).

8. The painting in the blue frame is a watercolor. The self-portrait does not have a blue frame. Since it is done in oils, it does not have a green frame (clue 2).

It does not have a red frame (clues 5 and 7). It must have a brown frame, so it hangs in the dining room (clue 3).

9. There is an oil painting in the kitchen. The painting in the kitchen does not have a green frame (clue 2) or a blue frame (clue 8). It must have a red frame, so it is the bowl of apples.

10. The lake painting is in the living room. If the painting in the den has a green frame (clue 2), then the lake painting has a blue frame. The farm painting must hang in the den in a green frame.

Makeover (Page 51)

Niecy's room is blue with a drama theme.
Kenshi's room is yellow with a sports theme.
Hannah's room is pink with a dance theme.
Samantha's room is green with a music theme.

Working Through the Clues

1. Samantha and Kenshi do not like pink. Neither Samantha nor Kenshi painted their room pink.

2. The girl with the yellow room is into sports. The room with the sports theme is yellow.

3. Niecy did not paint her room yellow. Niecy does not have a sports theme.

4. The girl with the music theme sings and plays piano.

5. Kenshi thinks the girl with the drama theme picked a pretty color. Kenshi does not have the room with the drama theme. The room with the drama theme is not pink (clue 1).

6. Hannah and the girl with the green room have dogs but no cats. Hannah's room is not green.

7. Niecy's brother and the girl who likes dance helped Niecy paint her room. Niecy does not have the room with the dance theme.

8. The girl with the blue room likes to sing, but she cannot play a musical instrument. The room with the music theme is not painted blue (clue 4).

9. The girl who picked the drama theme has a cat. Hannah does not have the drama-themed room.

10. The girl with the music theme and the girl with the pink room have sisters but no brothers. Niecy does not have a room with a music theme (clue 7), a sports theme (clue 3), or a dance theme (clue 7), so she has the drama-themed room. Niecy's room is not pink (clue 7). If Samantha and Kenshi do not have pink rooms (clue 1), then Hannah's room is pink. Hannah's room does not have a sports theme (clue 2).

11. Samantha's room is not yellow. If Niecy's room is not yellow (clue 3) and Hannah's room is pink (clue 10), then Kenshi has the yellow room with the sports theme.

12. The girl with the dance-themed room tried painting her room blue then changed her mind. If the dance-themed room is not blue, the sports-themed room is not blue (clue 2), and the music-themed room is not blue (clue 8), then Niecy's room with the drama theme is blue. Samantha must have chosen the only color and theme that are left, green and music.

Victory Lunch (Page 52)
James, in Seat A, Table One, had fish sticks.
Ben, in Seat B, Table One, had chili.
Bella, in Seat C, Table One, had a salad.
Lauren, in Seat D, Table One, had a hamburger.
Justin, in Seat A, Table Two, had chicken strips.
Alyssa, in Seat B, Table Two, had a hamburger.
Dylan, in Seat C, Table Two, had a veggie burger.
Mai, in Seat D, Table Two, had a salad.

Working Through the Clues
1. Two boys and two girls were at each table.
2. Both vegetarians were at the same table.
3. Two people ordered hamburgers and two people ordered salads, but only one hamburger and one salad was served at each table. At each table, a hamburger, salad, and two other meals were served.
4. James and Dylan are twins, but they don't like the same food. Dylan is a vegetarian. James and Dylan had different meals.
5. The person in seat A at Table One had fish sticks. The food served at Table One was a hamburger, salad, fish sticks, and one other meal.
6. The boy in seat A at Table Two had chicken strips. He did not have a winning time at the meet. The food served at Table Two was a hamburger, salad, chicken strips, and one other meal.
7. The girl who had the fastest time in freestyle had a hamburger. She sat at Table One.
8. Alyssa sat in seat B at Table Two. She did not have a salad.
9. The boy with the fastest time in backstroke had chili. None of the girls ordered chili.
10. James and Dylan sat at different tables.
11. At each table there was a girl who was eating a salad. None of the boys had a salad.
12. Unlike Table One, the girls at Table Two sat across from each other. A girl is in Seat D at Table Two. She is having a salad (clue 8).
13. Ben sat in Seat B across from a girl. If Ben sat across from a girl, he must have been seated at Table One (clue 12).
14. The boy who had the fastest time in breaststroke had a veggie burger. Both vegetarians sat at Table Two (clue 2). Dylan is a vegetarian (clue 4), so he

sat at Table Two. That means that James sat at Table One (clue 10). The meals at Table Two were a hamburger, salad, chicken strips, and a veggie burger. Dylan sat across from the boy in Seat A (clue 6), so he is in Seat C. The boy in Seat A must be Justin. In addition, if the boys had chicken strips and a veggie burger, and Alyssa did not have a salad (clue 8), she must have had a hamburger.
15. James did not have the winning time in any event. James did not have chili. If he did not have a salad (clue 11) or a hamburger (clue 7), then he is the boy in Seat A who had chicken strips (clue 6).
16. Lauren is the only girl to have a winning time. Her best friend, Bella, sat in Seat C. Lauren sat at Table One (clue 7). If Bella sat at Seat C, she must have been at Table One. If Lauren and Bella sat at Table One, then Mai sat at Table Two across from Alyssa (clue 11) in Seat D, and she ate a salad. If Bella is in Seat C, she is sitting across from James (clue 15). Lauren must be in Seat D (clue 13) across from Ben in Seat B. Lauren had a hamburger (clue 7), so Bella had a salad (clue 11).

Saturday Sundae (Page 53)
Micah had vanilla with hot fudge, whipped cream, and sprinkles.
Taylor had strawberry with sprinkles.
P.J. had chocolate with whipped cream and sprinkles.
Mom had vanilla with strawberry syrup.
Dad had chocolate with caramel and whipped cream.

Working Through the Clues
1. Three people had sprinkles.
2. Two people had chocolate ice cream, and two had vanilla ice cream. One person had strawberry.
3. Taylor and Mom were the only ones who did not have whipped cream. Micah, P.J., and Dad had whipped cream.
4. Micah was the only person who had three toppings. He did not have strawberry ice cream.
5. Mom and Taylor had one topping each. Mom was the only person who had strawberry syrup. P.J. and Dad had two toppings each (clue 4).
6. The person who had strawberry ice cream did not have any syrup.
7. Two people had chocolate ice cream with two toppings each. One had it with caramel. Since Mom only had one topping, she did not have chocolate ice cream (clue 5) or strawberry (clue 6). Mom had vanilla. If Micah had three toppings, he did not have chocolate ice cream or strawberry (clue 4). He had vanilla. P.J. and Dad had chocolate (clue 5). Taylor had strawberry ice cream (clue 5).
8. Taylor had sprinkles only.
9. Dad was not the person who had hot fudge.

10. P.J. had sprinkles. P.J. had chocolate ice cream (clues 7 and 8) with two toppings (clues 5 and 7), whipped cream (clue 3) and sprinkles. If that is so, then Dad, who also had chocolate ice cream and two toppings (clue 8), had caramel (clue 7) and whipped cream. That leaves Micah as the person who had hot fudge (clue 9) and the third and final person to have sprinkles (clues 1, 8, and 10).

Cool Cash (Page 54)

Total earned: $384

Fraction of total hours worked: Adrian ($\frac{1}{3}$), Kevin ($\frac{1}{3}$), Jason ($\frac{5}{24}$), Brandon ($\frac{1}{8}$)

Earnings per boy: Adrian ($128), Kevin ($128), Jason ($80), Brandon ($48)

Working Through the Clues:

1. Adrian and Kevin each worked eight Saturdays. They put in the most hours and made the most money.
2. The boys spent one hour every week at the Clarks for eight weeks. They worked a total of eight hours at the Clarks.
3. The customers paid 12 dollars per hour for the yard work, so the Clarks paid a total of 96 dollars.
4. Jason only worked the four Saturdays that the Goldbergs were scheduled. He worked fewer hours than Adrian and Kevin.
5. The boys spent two hours every week at the Onnessis for eight weeks. They worked sixteen hours at the Onnessis for a total of 192 dollars.
6. They spent two hours at the Goldbergs every other week. They worked eight hours at the Goldbergs for a total of 96 dollars. On the four Saturdays that the boys worked at the Goldbergs, Onnessis, and Clarks, they each put in five hours. On the four Saturdays they worked only at the Onnessis and Clarks, they each put in three hours. The total the boys earned over eight weeks was 384 dollars for 32 hours of yard work. Adrian and Kevin each worked 32 hours (clue 1). Jason worked 20 hours (clue 4).
7. Brandon only worked the four Saturdays that the Goldbergs were not scheduled. Brandon worked 12 hours altogether. The total number of work hours for the four boys combined was 96 hours. Adrian and Kevin each worked 32 hours or $\frac{32}{96}$ ($\frac{1}{3}$) of the total work hours. Jason worked 20 hours or $\frac{20}{96}$ ($\frac{5}{24}$) of the total work hours. Brandon worked 12 hours or $\frac{12}{96}$ ($\frac{1}{8}$) of the total work hours. Since there were never more than three boys working at any time, they each earned four dollars per hour (clue 3 and 4).

My Space (Page 55)

Leah's room is the largest.

Kathleen: 14 feet long, 14 feet wide, perimeter 56 feet, area 196 square feet

Eva: 14 feet long, 12 feet wide, perimeter 52 feet, area 168 square feet

Leah: 18 feet long, 12 feet wide, perimeter 60 feet, area 216 square feet

Abby: 16 feet long, 10 feet wide, perimeter 52 feet, area 160 square feet

Working Through the Clues:

1. Eva's room is two feet longer than wide. Eva's room is either 14 by 12 or 16 by 14.
2. The perimeter of Leah's room is four feet longer than the perimeter of Kathleen's room. Leah's room is larger than Kathleen's.
3. The second-largest room is square. The only length and width that are the same is 14 feet, so the second-largest room is 14 by 14. Its perimeter is 56 feet, and the square footage is 196 square feet. Neither Eva nor Leah have a square room (clues 1 and 2). Eva's room cannot be 14 feet wide, so it must be 14 by 12 (clue 1). That means the perimeter of her room is 52 feet, and the square footage is 168 feet.
4. The square footage of Abby's room is 160 square feet. Since the square footage of the square room is 196, Abby does not have the square room. That means that Kathleen has the square room.
5. Leah's room is 12 feet wide. If Leah's room is larger than Kathleen's (clue 2), then Leah's room must be 18 feet long. That means it has a perimeter of 60 feet and square footage of 216. Abby's room must be 16 feet long and ten feet wide with a perimeter of 52 feet.

In the Garden (Page 56)

First Row: lettuce (15 inches apart), 16 plants
Second Row: carrots (4 inches apart), 60 plants
Third Row: green peppers (18 inches apart), 13 plants
Fourth Row: cucumbers (1 foot apart), 20 plants
Fifth and Sixth Rows: tomatoes (3 feet apart), 7 plants in each row
Seventh and Eighth Rows: corn (1 foot apart), 20 plants in each row

Working Through the Clues:

1. The corn will grow the tallest.
2. The lettuce plants are 15 inches apart. If the rows are 20 feet long (240 inches), then there is room for 16 plants.
3. There are two rows of tomatoes.
4. The carrots are in the second row.

5. Cucumbers are planted one foot apart. There are at least 20 cucumber plants.

6. Rows seven and eight are for the tallest plants. Rows seven and eight are corn.

7. The plants in rows five and six are the same and about three feet apart. If there are two rows of corn (clue 5) and two rows of tomatoes (clue 3) then there can only be one row of each of the other vegetables. That means that there is one row of cucumbers with 20 plants (clue 4). The tomatoes must be in rows five and six. There are seven plants in each row.

8. Cucumbers and corn are planted the same distance apart (clue 5). Corn plants are planted one foot apart. There are two rows of corn (clue 6), each with 20 plants.

9. The plants in the third row are 18 inches apart. Cucumbers and lettuce are not in the third row (clues 2 and 4).

10. Carrots are planted four inches apart between the lettuce and the green peppers. If the carrots are between the lettuce and green peppers, the only possible row is row two. There are 60 plants in the row.

11. There are 13 plants in the third row (clue 11). The only plants that have not been counted are green peppers, so they must be in the third row. If there are 13 plants, then they must be 18 inches apart. If the carrots are between green peppers and lettuce, then lettuce is in row one. That means that the cucumbers are in row four.

Earth Friendly (Page 57)

Charlie's Team: 4 people, 92 pounds of trash, 20% cans, 35% glass, 20% plastic, 25% paper

Neville's Team: 6 people, 120 pounds of trash, 30% cans, 20% glass, 35% plastic, 15% paper

Yolanda's Team: 4 people, 96 pounds of trash, 20% cans, 25% glass, 20% plastic, 35% paper

Jenna's Team: 5 people, 110 pounds of trash, 15% cans, 30% glass, 25% plastic, 30% paper

Working Through the Clues:

1. Jenna's team was not the smallest. They collected twice the percentage of paper as Neville's, but half the percentage of cans.

2. Yolanda and Charlie had the same number of helpers on their teams, but Yolanda's picked up four more pounds of trash than Charlie's.

3. Each person on Charlie's team picked up an average of 23 pounds of trash.

4. There were six people on Neville's team, making it the largest. The other three teams had fewer than six people.

5. Charlie's team picked up a total of 92 pounds of trash. Thirty-five percent of it was made up of bottles and other glass. If each person picked up 23 pounds of trash, then there must be four people on Charlie's team. That means there are four people on Yolanda's team, and they collected 96 pounds of trash (clue 2). Jenna's team was not the smallest (clue 1) or the largest (clue 4), so there must have been five people on her team.

6. Jenna's team collected equal percentages of glass and paper and 15 percent cans. If Jenna's team collected half as many cans and twice as much paper as Neville's, then Neville collected 30 percent cans (clue 1).

7. Yolanda's team and Neville's team both picked up 24 pounds of glass. This is five percent more than the amount of paper Neville's team collected. Glass made up 25 percent of what Yolanda collected.

8. Charlie's team collected equal percentages of cans and plastic and 23 pounds of paper, ten pounds less paper than Jenna's team. Charlie's team collected 25 percent paper. If they collected 35 percent glass (clue 5), that leaves 40 percent divided evenly between cans and plastic, or 20 percent each.

9. Yolanda's team collected an equal percentage of cans and plastic.

10. Neville's team collected 35 percent plastic. Yolanda's team collected an equal amount in paper. If Neville also collected 30 percent cans (clue 6), that totals 65 percent, leaving 35 percent. If his team collected five percent more glass than paper (clue 7), that means they collected 20 percent glass and 15 percent paper. Jenna's team then collected 30 percent paper (clue 1). That means she also collected 30 percent glass (clue 6). That leaves Jenna 25 percent for plastic. Jenna collected 33 pounds of paper or 30 percent of her total (clue 6). That means her team collected 110 pounds of trash. If Neville's team collected 24 pounds of glass, which equaled 20 percent (clue 7), then Neville's team collected a total of 120 pounds of trash. Yolanda's team also collected 35 percent paper. That leaves 40 percent divided equally between cans and plastic, or 20 percent each (clue 9).

Blank Solution Grids

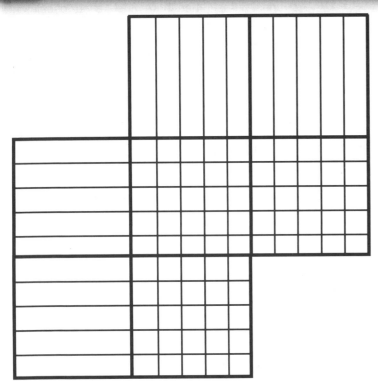

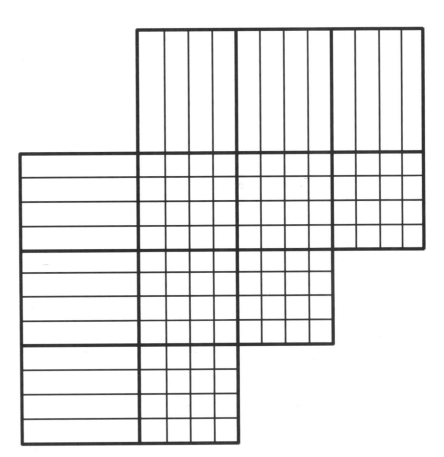